The Hyper-Creative Personality

First published in 2007 by New Holland Publishers (UK) Ltd
London • Cape Town • Sydney • Auckland
www.newhollandpublishers.com

10 9 8 7 6 5 4 3 2 1

Garfield House, 86–88 Edgware Road, London W2 2EA, UK
80 McKenzie Street, Cape Town 8001, South Africa
14 Aquatic Drive, Frenchs Forest, NSW 2086, Australia
218 Lake Road, Northcote, Auckland, New Zealand

ISBN 978 1 84537 615 4

Editorial Director: Jo Hemmings
Editors: Gareth Jones and Kate Parker
Assistant Editor: Giselle Osborne
Design: Adam Morris
Cover design: Ian Hughes, Mousemat Design Ltd
Production: Hema Gohil

Cover reproduction by Pica Digital PTE Ltd, Singapore.
Printed and bound in India by Replika Press Pvt. Ltd.

The Hyper-Creative Personality

How to focus your ideas and become the most successful person you know

BLAIRE PALMER

NEW HOLLAND

CONTENTS

INTRODUCTION

THE HYPER-CREATIVE PERSONALITY

Reading through the report, I knew it was accurate:

- You may be interested in the overall plan and will not spend too much time gathering detailed facts.
- You rely on your 'sixth sense' to tell you what is right.
- People find it hard to follow some of your moves.
- You can be a little impulsive and rush into judgements too quickly.

A colleague had done my Margerison-McCann Team Management Profile test[1], as part of her training with the tool. I am sure she learnt a lot with me as her case study. But I am sure I learnt more.

The overall themes resonated with me strongly. As I looked at my scores, I thought, 'No wonder I can't seem to get around to my paperwork, that so many of my ideas remain incomplete. That explains why I get a tight knot in my stomach when I have to carry out repetitive tasks.' I was proud that my enjoyment of, and talent for, ideas had been recognized and printed clearly in black and white for all to see. But I was concerned to read about the flip-side and how it could be holding me back.

And in the following weeks, as I continued to work with clients in my creative thinking and executive coaching business – successful, creative, outgoing people like myself – I noticed the same traits in many of them. Some were more introverted than me, others more organized. But they all struggled with seemingly simple and yet vital aspects of their job, while excelling in others, just as I did.

These people were not just creative. Yes, they had ideas. But other factors combined with their creativity and resulted in an explosive mix of behaviours. Their true value to their organization was being limited by their own actions.

When I first coined the term 'Hyper-Creative' as a distinct personality type (that is, more than just a creative person with a deadline problem), I thought that its associated behaviours and thinking processes were relatively rare. While there are plenty of creative people in the business world, I assumed that the particular combination of working preferences I connected with Hyper-Creatives accounted for a pretty small proportion of the total employed population.

Perhaps I wanted to believe that we Hyper-Creatives were an endangered species, or, more likely, that people with our extraordinary talents were few and far between and therefore should be especially prized by our employers. But I was wrong. It just goes to show you how relying on your gut-feeling to the exclusion of the facts can be a dangerous habit. I was reluctant to change my theory because, frankly, I had already made up my mind. But the evidence, on this occasion, shouted louder than my intuitive assumptions and won the day.

The reality is that all of us, at some time or other, behave as Hyper-Creatives. A particular type of project, a peculiar combination of forces in our life, a certain mood, or the influence of other people, can bring out the Hyper-Creative in us all. We get an idea, start a project with gusto, get overwhelmed or simply bored with it after a period of time and fail to finish what we began. Sound familiar? Well some people are like this on occasion. Others are like this the majority of the time. And a few are like this almost exclusively.

So, what is a Hyper-Creative? A more complete definition can be found in the next chapter, but because you are probably a little impatient, I will explain briefly here.

Hyper-Creative people are full of ideas. They don't just see a problem – they see numerous ways to fix it. They enjoy the generation of imaginative solutions. They invent new products, new businesses, new processes. They get a thrill from using their creative abilities.

But how is a Hyper-Creative person different to a person who is simply creative? Creativity in itself is not a problem. In fact it is highly prized in business. The problem with Hyper-Creatives occurs when their creativity is combined with some other personality traits resulting in some, or all, of the following behaviours:

- Impatience with detailed, systematic work.
- Neglecting facts and data in preference for gut-feeling and intuitive decision-making.
- Passion at the thinking and imagining stage but a low boredom threshold when it comes to putting ideas into action.
- Difficulty following a project through to completion.
- Swings in temperament from great highs to significant lows.
- Flexibility around deadlines meaning projects are rarely finished on time or are rushed at the final stage.
- Sheer quantity of ideas, which can overwhelm the individual themselves and other people around them.
- Difficulty distinguishing good ideas from bad ideas.
- Absolute conviction about the right course of action (and the ability to persuade others of this) without the necessary research and foundations to back up the plan.

The definitions I have used in this book will help you to identify whether you have a propensity to operate in a Hyper-Creative way the majority of the time. If you don't, some of the descriptions may not resonate with you so strongly. The tips, examples and advice will still be of use, but you may not feel you can blame Hyper-Creativity for all your troubles. Sorry.

My intention with this book is to spark your ideas. It isn't a self-help book in the traditional sense. There are no exercises to complete. There are no boxes to tick. There are no direct calls to action, in fact. This is intentional. Creative people do not need to be told exactly how to achieve an outcome. In fact, we will find it patronizing and, in any case, for us the fun is being inspired by a raw concept and working it up into something fresh and suitable for our own circumstances.

Also, Hyper-Creatives find it hard to finish what they start. So, while exercises at the end of every chapter might appeal to you when you first begin to use this book, my suspicion is that halfway through you will stop doing the exercises, feel you cannot continue reading without completing the prescribed action steps, get disillusioned and not finish the book. I want you to finish the book, so I've tried to make the process as effortless as possible.

This does not mean reading the book is enough. In order to change the results you get in your life you will need to change your behaviours. But exactly how you do this is up to you. Experiment, try concepts on for size, see what works and what doesn't. When I work with clients who want to develop their creative thinking skills, each one takes something unique away from the process. The variety of ways to use the advice and help in this book is endless and, just as my clients do, I hope each reader will interpret the ideas here in their own unique way.

One of the reasons I changed my original definition of Hyper-Creativity was as a result of talking to my case studies. I have known some of these people for many years. I know from their behaviours that they are Hyper-Creative. And yet, when the results of their personality assessments came back, a few clearly Hyper-Creative people did not meet the very narrow definition I had originally created. So it was back to the drawing board. The result was a more inclusive definition (which I explain fully in Chapter 1) and therefore a concept that would have relevance for more people.

My choice of case studies was intentional, too. I could have approached high profile business people who would probably meet the Hyper-Creative criteria but who have overcome their weaknesses and achieved great success as a result. People like Richard Branson and Jamie Oliver would probably qualify. These are 'ideas' people. They are always working on an exciting project, embarking on an adventure (a word many Hyper-Creatives use), popping up doing something so unexpected that it has become the norm for them. Maybe it would have been useful to hear how they managed their excitement over shiny new ideas and were able to finish what they started despite their natural tendency to be distracted by the next opportunity. But there were many reasons I did not choose this route.

Firstly, there are plenty of books written about entrepreneurs. If you want to know how to turn your business idea into a multi-million pound concern you have a huge choice already.

Secondly, not all Hyper-Creatives run their own businesses. In fact, few do. They work somewhere in the ranks of a corporation, in the public sector, in a small family operation, for a charity. They may be a high-flyer on the fast-track to the top. They may not. I did not want to suggest that entrepreneurs and Hyper-Creatives were the same thing or that the best place for people with these preferences was running their own company.

In fact, there is a huge need for creative people in all areas of the working world. I am motivated by two powerful forces:

1. To help people understand themselves better and develop their innate strengths, interests and creativity, so that they can achieve their full potential. Knowing that you have talent but being unable to express it is frustrating, de-energizing and, ultimately, leads to an unsatisfactory life.
2. To bring real creative thinking into business. Many organizations think they do this already, but most find a specific time and a place for ideas rather than allowing creativity, open, uncensored problem-solving and free-thinking to interfere too much with day-to-day working.

Yes, it is tempting to go it alone when your particular talents seem unappreciated and your work environment seems to suffocate fresh approaches. But, unless you have found a way to finish what you start and turn your ideas into action, starting your own company could be a very costly experiment.

Thirdly, I wanted the case studies to be people we can all identify with. These aren't people who have solved the problem of being Hyper-Creative. They are people who are figuring it out. They have some excellent ideas which have worked for them and which could inspire you. But they haven't got it sussed – not yet anyway.

I really appreciated their honesty in our conversations. And I hope you will too.

CHAPTER ONE

HELP – I THINK I MIGHT BE HYPER-CREATIVE

You've been up half the night. You just had to get started. The idea that came to you while you were staring at the bedroom ceiling at 3am was just too good to forget about. I mean, what would have happened if Einstein had his brainwave about relativity at four in the morning, told himself, 'Oh, I'll think more about that tomorrow,' and when he woke up all he could remember was that E equalled something?

So you got out of bed and headed straight for your laptop. Wasting no time, you started writing the proposal, the business plan or the letter to the Institute of Nanotechnology. It felt great. Your blood was pumping, the creativity was flowing and simultaneously five per cent of your brain was working on your Nobel Peace Prize acceptance speech. Finally, with the groundwork complete, you went to bed, a satisfied smile across your face.

But this morning, in the cold light of day, the doubts have started to appear. Perhaps you shared your idea with your partner or a colleague and they asked some ignorant question like: 'Have you thought about how much that would cost?' Maybe you did a bit more research and discovered your unique concept is already on the market and making millions for some other brain-box. Or maybe you just realized how much work it would take to turn your insight into reality.

Over the coming days or weeks your initial zeal wanes as more and more obstacles appear to sabotage your project. What started as a fresh, shiny, exciting new chapter becomes a boring slog, an additional burden, a 'should' rather than a 'want to'. And eventually, with the odds against success stacking up, you admit defeat and shelve the whole thing.

If this tale resonates with you, you will know that there is a sequel. Because next week, next month or next year, some other flight of fancy will pop in to your head, even better than the last, and the cycle will repeat. And repeat. And repeat.

Just like a Mills and Boon novel, the character names may change but the story line is basically the same. You get a great idea. You feel incredibly excited and motivated. You tell everyone about it and take the initial steps towards realizing its potential. Then you lose steam and focus. You become bogged down and bored by the mundane, detailed implementation stage. You start to see the flaws in the project and all the obstacles ahead. Eventually, you stop working on it altogether. And then you have another brilliant idea. And the whole process begins again.

I'm not a mind reader. I know about this for two reasons:

1. As a creative thinking partner and executive coach for business leaders, teams and entrepreneurs, I have thousands of hours of experience helping people just like this. (Not all of my clients have this particular challenge. Some use my services to help them originate better ideas, to become more creative. But many experience the pattern described above.)
2. I am one. There, I said it. And I am glad that is off my chest before we go any further.

You see, somewhere, stuffed in the darkest corner of my office, lies many a half completed book proposal, business idea and project plan. An idea will come from nowhere and be just too good to ignore. Except that, after a few days or weeks, that's exactly what happens.

I have always been what I flatteringly call a 'self-starter'. The problem is I've always struggled to be a 'self-finisher'. Of course, not every project I begin is left incomplete. I finished my degree. I qualified as an executive coach. My clients know I will meet their deadlines. I finished this book (you can flick to the back to check if you like).

But my tendency is to have far more ideas and start far more projects than I can ever finish. For much of my life my completion rate was embarrassingly low – for every idea that came to fruition there are 10, maybe 100, under my floorboards that died prematurely. And the same applies to my clients, all of whom are successful in business or in the corporate world. On more than one occasion they must have finished what they started in order to be where they are today. But turning a brilliant concept into a completed task is troublesome for these highly creative individuals, who know that it's pretty much all downhill after the initial flash of inspiration.

It is probably true for you, too. Whether you work for yourself, for a corporation or in the public sector, you've had moments of triumph – an idea that you took from A to Z. Then there are all the bright ideas that fell by the wayside. Some just didn't hold water and were rejected consciously. But others had within them true potential to transform the world, the country, your company, your team or your life. And what happened to them?

That's the downside. What's the upside?

Not everyone is like this by the way. The shelves at the bookshop (in fact, probably all the titles to the left and the right of this volume) are heaving with weighty tomes intended to spark the reader's creative juices. While you have ideas pouring out of your pores, some people don't operate that way. Many wish they could.

You will remember that meeting where the CEO asked for original contributions and everyone but you bowed their head, eyes on their agendas, in the hope they wouldn't be called on to share. They had nothing. But you relished the opportunity to brainstorm, create, hoist your ideas up the flagpole to see if anyone saluted.

You have a gift that is highly prized. Ideas are your currency. Your ability to originate ideas is one of the key assets you bring to your work. Sure, this gift causes you some sleepless nights... and causes your colleagues, friends and family to feel mildly frustrated with you on occasion. But if you could harness the power of your ideas, find a way to sift through the detritus and select those with real potential – and then follow them through to completion – you could vastly improve your levels of success, both professionally and personally.

As a result of the time spent working with people like you, and challenging myself to address this same flaw in me, I have identified some of the common characteristics of this personality and pulled together a set of strategies to minimize its negative impact and maximize its potential. Using these strategies is how I wrote this book while the other half-baked ideas came to nothing.

And they helped Sophie too:

Case Study – 'Sophie'

I realized that detailed work was not for me quite early on, when I was meant to work for one week in a 'fax room', checking faxes and telephoning people to collect them. I vowed on the Tuesday that I would never do anything like that again. I could have killed myself in that job. I didn't make it to the end of the week.

These days I bring someone onto the project who is good at the parts I find boring. We had an objective setting day recently and I had a very clear understanding of the big picture and where we were going. But I was too focused on that to think about the format of the day itself. One of my colleagues is perfect for that. She is not a reflector. She is practical, delivery-focused and she did it very effectively. I have learnt to focus on my bit and leave her to do hers. When I am thrown in with people like that I can begin to lose interest and switch off, which is probably a really bad thing. It's better for me to let her get on with it. I know when I am getting on someone's nerves and I know when to back off.

By inviting someone with different strengths and areas of interest to work on a project with her, Sophie has minimized the negative impact of her boredom with detail. Her current job gives her the opportunity to use her creative mind – the job in the fax office did not – but there are always parts of a job that are not your natural preference. Instead of forcing herself to work in a way that did not suit her or bring out her best, she delegated to someone who was perfectly suited to the task.

Later in the book we'll be looking at this strategy and others like it in more detail. While not all of them will appeal to you, taking onboard one or two may help you eliminate the extremes that you are sometimes guilty of and capitalize on your fertile imagination.

The first step is to understand what makes you this way.

A bit about personality profiling

In order to understand what makes you operate in this way and, ultimately, how to use this behaviour to your advantage, it is valuable to know a little about personality profiling.

Most of us have completed a personality profiling questionnaire like the Myers-Briggs Type Indicator[2]. These assessments are intended to give you an insight into your personality type. They measure the ways you naturally prefer to operate as opposed to your learnt strengths.

The assumption these tools make (which I am also making here) is that all of us have different preferences and innate areas of greater potential. For instance, some people have a more extrovert character, while others are more introvert. It might be your colleague's preference to go away and think through an argument before making her mind up. It might be your style to talk through a problem to gain clarity and refine your view.

Some people are 'straight-line thinkers', others 'scattered thinkers'. Perhaps your partner is someone that makes and maintains daily to-do lists, while you will doodle and mind-map when you are planning your day.

And some people are ideas people while others have the ability to take someone else's idea and make it work.

While we can learn to have abilities in areas that are not our preference, we will never be able to change our core preferences. Here is an example:

Case study – 'Miranda'

I used to be a loans officer for a bank. I had to sit at a desk and review balance sheets. I had to tell people they could not have their cheques paid. I had to write loads of detailed reports. All the interviews with customers were negative. I ended up doing the job for eight months and it was awful.

When I have to do work that doesn't fit with my natural preferences I get a bit low, actually. I don't feel motivated and I find it really hard to concentrate on what I have to do. Let's take invoicing – it doesn't take me long when I get to it but I can't get started with it. It's boring.

For me there is no effort in 'creating'. I can sit there and talk about ideas and concepts and it isn't work at all. Then I get to the organizing part, resources, people, time-tabling. It's at that point that I start thinking, 'This is hard work!'

Miranda's story demonstrates what happens when you try to work in ways that are not to your preference. This is not to say you should never challenge yourself and address a weakness. Many of the success strategies in this book will look at ways you can teach yourself techniques that do not come naturally, but will help you to capitalize on your strengths.

However, it does also demonstrate that the more time you spend outside of your areas of preference, the more dissatisfied, stressed and bored you are going to become.

When I was at school I was strong in the creative subjects like English and Music but weak in the sciences. My teachers advised me to focus on the subjects where I was struggling most so my parents paid for Maths and Science tutoring for me. When the exam results came through they were what we might describe as mediocre. My English and Music grades were far lower than anticipated and my Maths and Science grades were exceedingly average. This taught me a couple of important lessons:

1. I should give up on my ambitions to become a vet like James Herriot *in All Creatures Great and Small* (you need Biology).
2. I would never again neglect my strengths in order to focus purely on my weaknesses.

Unfortunately, we live in a culture where much more emphasis is put on our weaknesses and failures than on our strengths and successes. Although most of us are aware of the power of acknowledgement and praise, most of us are far more familiar with criticism. Teachers, bosses and parents are generally more concerned with helping us fix what we don't do well than with celebrating what we can do well and encouraging us to pursue it.

And when one has a behavioural pattern as described at the beginning of this chapter (great ideas that rarely come to fruition) it is natural for those around us to try to change us. Why can't we just finish what we start? Why are we so lazy and why do we get put off at the first sign of hard work? Why don't we keep our bright ideas to ourselves until we've done some of the groundwork and established whether they have the potential to really work?

These are all good, honest questions. And I will tell you why it is hard for us.

The Hyper-Creative personality

Artists, actors and musicians are renowned for it. The 'creative personality' is associated with emotional highs followed by crashing lows, dramatic over-reactions and real or perceived bouts of depression. When actresses blub uncontrollably as they receive their Oscar, we aren't surprised: that's the creative temperament for you. When rock stars set out on a self-destructive rampage, it's all put down to them being 'the creative type'. And when poets spiral into a deep malaise, we know that it's all part of the curse of being creative. But what has any of this got to do with you?

You are what I call 'Hyper-Creative'.

What that means is you have many of the characteristics associated

'Ideas can be highly distracting... They almost always come in the middle of the night'

with artistic people. (You also have many of the characteristics associated with entrepreneurs... if that appeals to you more.) You may not be much cop with a number two sable paint brush, but coming up with ideas is very much an art form for you.

It is hard to say where your inspiration comes from. Just as a painter is inspired by life – people he sees on the train, emotions he feels, memories from his childhood – you are inspired by random objects or events. You can never switch it off. Whatever you are doing – reading a magazine, watching TV, taking a walk – you could suddenly get a bolt from the blue. That's when your cycle kicks in.

The painter would rush to his studio and start slapping oils about. You probably head for the nearest computer, scrap of paper or even jot down a few salient points on the back of your hand.

These ideas can be highly distracting. They rarely come when you've got time to work on them, when you have set aside a morning to just think. They almost always come when you have a deadline, when you are meant to be enjoying quality time with your family or in the middle of the night.

Just like a hyperactive child, you aren't in complete control at these times. It is incredibly difficult to ignore the new idea jumping loop-the-loop in your head.

While you might have the discipline to hold yourself back for a few hours, at some point in the short term you will almost certainly start scoping out your idea. Until you've done so you won't be able to do much else.

And just like a hyperactive child who races madly round the house, practically bouncing off the walls for three hours, only to collapse in an exhausted heap or break down in tears following their exertions, your high is eventually followed by the low, when the reality of the project, the gaping holes in the concept or the sheer amount of slog needed bring you back to earth.

'Remember the time you were going to apply for that patent for your revolutionary invention?'

And that's why I have termed this personality type Hyper-Creative. In a sense you have too many ideas. Ask anyone who knows you well (particularly if they are not like this themselves) and they will admit that sometimes (if they are being polite) you do get a bit carried away with your ideas before you've done the ground work. They will cite examples – remember the time you were going to apply for that patent for your revolutionary invention or the time you were going to write that book? They'll recount in uncomfortable detail how your initial enthusiasm eventually waned... and how you do that a lot.

Maybe you've only just started to realize that this is your pattern. Maybe you haven't really acknowledged how great you are with ideas in comparison with most people and how that can be detrimental to your overall success. And perhaps you wish you could just concentrate on what you are doing at the time you are doing it and only have your next idea when you've finished what you started.

So a preference for creative thinking, a way with ideas, a mind that enjoys inventing and problem-solving are all part of the Hyper-Creative personality. But that's not all.

The science bit

In order to clarify whether you are Hyper-Creative or not, you will need to consider four different aspects of your personality:

Your preferred thinking style: Do you process ideas by talking them through aloud or by thinking them through in your head? Are you more extrovert or introvert?

How you deal with ideas: Are you more practical and focused on facts and details, or are you more creative, preferring possibilities and future-orientated ideas?

How you make decisions: Do you analyze the data and carry out your research before making a decision, or do you rely on gut-feeling?

How you organize yourself and others: Are you quite structured, interested in processes and systems, or do you take a more flexible approach whereby you change direction, change your mind or change the deadline?

Highly Hyper-Creative – the definition

Put simply, the classic Hyper-Creative individual is extroverted, very creative, makes decisions based on their gut feelings, and is flexible in their organizational style.

What I mean by extrovert is that they enjoy talking. By talking they get clarity. They get to hear other people's opinions, which can spark them further. They may do some initial working alone, but then they will want to tell people about it.

The creative part speaks for itself. They prefer having their own ideas to developing other people's ideas. Although they might be expert at practical tasks, this will normally be because they have taught themselves these skills rather than because they are naturally practical.

And then there is the gut-feeling element, also referred to in this book as being 'beliefs-driven'. You generally know what you think, what you feel and what you like. You know that an idea is a good one before you've got the data to prove it. And, if you are highly beliefs-driven, you will either gather data that supports your view (while ignoring the rest) or you will not gather data at all. That's why when someone asks you 'How much would it cost?' you have no idea, and possibly think the question pretty irrelevant.

The flexible element is partly what causes the trouble. Highly Hyper-Creative people tend not to be organized by nature. Their ideas go off in many unstructured directions rather than in a straight, logical line. Flexibility is partly why they are able to see possibilities where others do not. But it also has a cost.

So, that is the definition of a highly Hyper-Creative person. If this description fits you perfectly, then you are probably getting a sense of how this combination of being extrovert, creative, beliefs-driven and flexible affects your ability to see projects through, meet dead-lines, deal with detail and relate to other people.

But what if you don't totally recognize this description? Parts of it resonate with you, but something is not quite right. Well, this is because not all Hyper-Creatives are exactly like this.

Hyper-Creative – a more inclusive definition

In my research into Hyper-Creativity I spoke to many people who exhibited Hyper-Creative behaviours but did not conform to the definition above. They all had a preference for creative tasks over practical ones. But not all were beliefs-driven *and* flexible. Some were one or the other. Indeed, I have experienced almost all of the problems that Hyper-Creativity can lead to and yet I am very structured and organized. So something in the definition wasn't quite right. It became clear to me that only one of beliefs-driven and flexible was needed in order to turn creativity from a pure gift into a self-limiting burden.

In my experience, both introverts and extroverts can be Hyper-Creative. Extroversion can make your failure to follow through more public (because you told everyone about the idea, set up an expectation that it was going to happen and then bailed on it); introverts go through the same process, just more privately.

What really matters is the combination of beliefs-driven, analytical, flexible and structured preferences.

It is the beliefs-driven bit and the flexible bit that gets us Hyper-Creatives into trouble. If you have one or both in your profile (as well as being creative) then you are Hyper-Creative.

So there are six types of Hyper-Creative:

1. Introvert / Creative / Beliefs-driven / Flexible

2. Extrovert / Creative / Beliefs-driven / Flexible

3. Introvert / Creative / Analytical / Flexible

4. Extrovert / Creative / Analytical / Flexible

5. Introvert / Creative / Beliefs-driven / Structured

6. Extrovert / Creative / Beliefs-driven / Structured

Those creative types who are both analytical and structured may connect with some of what is in this book. However, your preference for analyzing data and structuring yourself and others means that you avoid some of the greatest pitfalls of being Hyper-Creative and, therefore, I'm afraid I can't extend this term to you! But it's still worth reading on. There will be times when you operate in a more flexible and beliefs-driven way and, at those times, some of the tips here could get you out of a sticky situation!

How different Hyper-Creatives operate... briefly
We've already looked at the classic extrovert / creative / beliefs-driven / flexible Hyper-Creative (see page 21). These people are talkative, full of ideas, guided in their decision-making by their gut feelings and tend to be disorganized (or 'differently-organized', if you prefer!).

Introvert / creative / beliefs-driven / flexible Hyper-Creatives
These people are much the same, but they do their processing in their heads rather than aloud. In this context, introvert does not mean shy and extrovert outgoing. It refers to the way we think about ideas and information. An introvert Hyper-Creative will disappear

for a week to work on her idea and won't tell you what it is until she's ready... or more likely until she's gone off it!

Introvert or extrovert / creative / analytical / flexible Hyper-Creatives:

These people have an interest in data – the facts – which is rather useful. It helps them legitimize their ideas and demonstrate how they can work in practice. By the time they get bored of an idea, enough other people may be convinced of its worth to do the implementation themselves.

Extrovert / analytical Hyper-Creatives will want to talk about the facts, maybe boring others silly with bits of information they have discovered and, the more they talk, the more those bits of information lead to creative connections, which in turn leads them to talk even more. Introvert / analytical Hyper-Creatives will stay up late absorbing fat tomes of information and making creative connections in their head every time they read a new fact.

Being analytical is helpful, but these Hyper-Creatives are still flexible, which means they can lose track of deadlines, have a disorganized nature and not realize when the time for exploring is over and the time for decisive action has begun.

Extrovert / creative / beliefs-driven / structured Hyper-Creatives

I am one of these. I tend to think in quite straight, logical lines and prefer to make lists than make mind-maps, which I find disorientating. Being structured is also one of the reasons I can help flexible Hyper-Creatives. I understand what they are going through but, by bringing my more structured mind to the problem, we can find a way forward together. For instance, I can remind even my most flexible clients of the deadlines they have set and keep them focused on their goals.

Introvert / creative / beliefs-driven / structured Hyper-Creatives

These people are similar but, while people like me are calling all their friends, family and vague acquaintances to tell them excitedly about their latest brainwave, the introvert / creative /

beliefs-driven / structured Hyper-Creative is madly making pages of notes describing the steps needed to get started with their idea.

In both of the last two cases, it is the beliefs-driven part that causes some trouble, because decisions are based on gut feelings, which may or may not be accurate. We are not that interested in getting the facts. Why bother? We already know the answer.

Which type are you? If you are a gut-feeling, beliefs-driven type. then you probably already know. If not, Chapter Three will provide you with even more data, which will leave you in no doubt.

Preferences and emphases

There are two other important points to mention here:

Firstly, you will notice I've talked a lot about 'preferences' as opposed to 'strengths' and 'weaknesses'. This is because having a preference is not the same as being good at something. If you have devoted a great deal of time and effort to becoming a genius researcher, for instance, you may assume you are naturally analytical rather than beliefs-driven, which may not be the case. You may get a great deal of satisfaction from completing research, from gathering data and finding sources of information. But this may be a skill you have learnt. Your satisfaction could be coming from doing a job well rather than because you have an innate preference for that kind of task. One clue as to your true preference might be that, at the same time as carrying out the research, you also have a strong gut-feeling about what the research will prove. However hard you try not to jump to conclusions, often the research you carry out will confirm what you already knew at an intuitive level.

Sometimes our natural preferences and operating style can be 'knocked out of us' or forced into hiding by a society that values something else. Part of the process of developing as a Hyper-Creative is about embracing your preferences and working on them so that they become your strengths.

Secondly, no one is always creative or always practical, just as no one is always analytical or always beliefs-driven.

All of us have a preference, at times, for behaviours that seem completely contrary to our usual ways of operating. In certain circumstances, even the most extrovert person will want to take themselves off somewhere for a solitary think. This is just as innate as their predominant preference for extroversion. In fact, extroverts sometimes desire solitude more than introverts. When they are in public, they very often feel like they are 'putting on a show'. In sharing their thoughts, feelings, ideas and stories in a communal environment, they can become quite exhausted. Their alone time and quiet thinking time is almost sacred.

The same applies whatever your predominant preference. A beliefs-driven decision maker may revert to an analytical style for specific types of problem, for instance money matters. In every other aspect of their life they may go with their feelings, but when it comes to securing their financial future, they might want a low-risk, guaranteed outcome, and may go through their options with a fine-tooth comb.

Equally, flexibly organized individuals may seek structure in some aspect of their lives. While everything else they do might be subject to last-minute changes, completing the newspaper's daily Sudoku puzzle or watching a favourite TV programme might be an immovable part of their routine.

And this is a 'Good Thing'. It means that you not only have the ability but, under certain conditions, have a preference for non-Hyper-Creative ways of operating. Understanding when, why and how this manifests itself will be important later on when we start looking at how to manage yourself more effectively.

It's also useful to get a sense of how extreme or subtle your preferences are. You might be nearly equally balanced in your preference for creative and practical tasks. And you might be extreme in one category: e.g. highly flexible or highly beliefs-driven.

Then, of course, you could suspect you have a highly pronounced preference in all four of the elements mentioned, in which case you really need to make this book a project you finish!

Thinking about 'preferences' rather than strengths, and 'emphasis' rather than black or white categories, is an important starting point. It will help you decide which of the strategies in this book are most suited to you. If you are very high-end, extrovert, creative, flexible and beliefs-driven, you will find it very difficult to adapt your style. It may be more useful for you to focus only on what comes naturally to you and build around you a support team of people who can do everything else.

However, if you find yourself somewhere in the middle and perhaps prefer structured or analytical tasks, you may enjoy strategies such as 'Leading the horse to water' in Chapter Eight (see page 109).

Okay, that's enough background. There's a lot more to know about these different types and the pros and cons of each, but we'll leave that until Chapter Three (see page 36). I can see your eyes glazing over already. We Hyper-Creatives can be so impatient!

So, you are probably already asking, 'When is she going to tell me what to do about this?'

Well, the answer is now.

CHAPTER TWO

FROM CHAOS TO CLARITY

What is the purpose of this book? Is it:

1. To teach you to be less Hyper-Creative and more like everyone else?
2. To show you how to have better ideas so that the fact you hardly ever finish what you start can be overlooked by those in authority, because you are seen as the mad, irreverent genius in the corner, who doesn't have to play by the same rules as everyone else?
3. To help you turn your Hyper-Creativity into an asset while managing the extremes that turn it into a curse?

No prizes for guessing that it is primarily 3., although there are elements of 1. and 2. in this book too – so whatever you guessed you were right! Well done!

CHILD'S PLAY

You can probably trace your Hyper-Creativity back to childhood. Try thinking back to a time before education, peer pressure, cultural influences and the desire for financial security clouded your judgement, you probably acted in a way that was purely Hyper-Creative. In other words, you were probably much more your 'authentic self' than you are today.

When you were six years old, how did you spend your free time? Like most kids you probably had an active imaginary life in which you were a cowboy, a police officer, a princess or a vet. I spent many a happy afternoon wrapping my cuddly toys in toilet paper and laying them side by side on the bed to recover from their various injuries. And chances are you had a similarly all-consuming fantasy too. Otherwise it's just me.

Children make up games, they invent scenarios, they are inspired by what they see around them and incorporate that into their play. They do not censor their games because they have become too unrealistic, and often children work together to develop the original idea, building on each other's suggestions and letting the game evolve.

By the age of 25–30 months, children are able to develop stories, create pretend worlds and co-operate with each other to embellish their initial ideas. The development of these abilities coincides with two other important realizations – that what they think isn't always what others think, and that it is possible to put themselves in another person's shoes.[3]

I don't want to idealize child's play. After all, little kids lack some of the highly advanced communication skills and insights that are so helpful to us adults when it comes to working with other people on a creative task. When child's play gets out of hand there are likely to be tears and fighting, something which you wouldn't see at your average board meeting… although, hang on a minute… maybe children and adults aren't so different after all.

However, if we consider child's play when it is going well, it incorporates many of the elements of a great brainstorming session:

- The freedom to express your ideas, no matter how off-the-wall they are.
- The lack of time pressure and deadlines, allowing an idea to spiral, without the need to reach a pre-ordained target by a specific time.
- The willingness to listen to others and 'play' with ideas.

Chances are, if you suspect you are Hyper-Creative today, the roots of that can be seen in your past. Maybe you loved make-believe and dressing up. Maybe you had a series of make-a-quick-buck ideas such as selling soda-stream lime cordial from your garden gate or charging friends to have a go on your new bike. Maybe you locked yourself away for hours on end, inventing futuristic modes of transport or designing wacky clothes that the people of the 21st century would be wearing (all gold lamé with in-built radiation deflectors or some such).

So, what happens to all that raw creativity? Basically, the natural curiosity that motivates children to ask, 'But why?', 'But how?' and 'But why?' again is educated out of us. Adults undervalue creativity in children by:

- Teaching them that there is a 'correct' way of doing things, which undermines the child's natural urge to experiment.
- Pressuring children, at a certain age, to be realistic – for example, labelling outlandish fantasies as 'silly'.
- Comparing children with one another and subtly encouraging them to conform to a certain set of rules or values (thus stifling the creative processes involved in breaking away from the 'norm').
- Discouraging curiosity, perhaps simply as a result of frustration with the constant questioning (and because they don't actually know why you can't build a house on a cloud and why fish turn upside-down when they die).[4]

Case Study – 'Adrian'

Dad had this expression called 'footling'. Have you heard of footling? No, no-one has. But I would footle. That means to fuss about, waste time. I wouldn't be able to concentrate or get on with things. My dad made me a list, which consisted of 7am: get up, 7.10am: clean teeth, etc. And it went all the way up to 8.30am when it was time to go to school and then it went out the window.

After 8.30am, there was no list and I didn't know what I was meant to be doing. I guess my Dad was trying to give me some structure, but without him doing it for me it all fell apart.

I am a dreamer but that was never seen as a good thing. It was always seen as wasting time. I am never going to be like everyone else and keep my head down. I couldn't possibly do it.

Of course it's a cop-out to blame the adults who influenced us as children for discounting the importance of childhood creativity. They learnt these lessons from the influential adults in their lives and those influential adults learnt it in the same way.

In any case, that creativity is still very much part of you: you can't help it, despite this pressure to conform. You might not have much freedom to explore your creativity in your work at the moment. You may not know how to handle your super-powers and they may manifest themselves in a way that is inconsistent, unreliable and sometimes frustrating to you and to others. And you may feel that what's really valued by your employer is attention to detail, process, structure and meeting targets on time, not radical new ways to transform the organization.

So, you have three options (which are remarkably similar to the three options at the start of this chapter):

1. Admit defeat. Try to blend in. The world doesn't need more creative people who can't finish what they start. The most sensible thing to do is to ignore the ideas when they come to you and just get on with doing what you are paid to do.
2. Do nothing. This is the way you are, and other people can just like it or lump it. Anyway, you were never that interested in getting to the top of your profession. Leave that to the bland suits.
3. Work on your strengths. Make them irresistible, reliable, powerful and valuable. Find ways of minimizing the impact of your weaknesses.

Well, obviously, the answer is 3. Because if you're reading this book you've probably already tried 1. and 2. and it hasn't been satisfactory for you. You want to be yourself. You don't want to be like everyone else. You couldn't be

'The ability to generate new ideas is one of the key elements of business success'

like them even if you did want to. And actually you do want to get to the top. You want to see what you are capable of.

And that's why my approach is to focus mainly on 3. I want you to tap back into your childhood preferences for imaginative play and, at the same time, develop the emotional intelligence you lacked back then (self-awareness, self-management, empathy, the ability to relate effectively with others etc.).

But, apart from making you more fulfilled, why is this important?

CREATIVITY AND BUSINESS

You are actually a highly prized commodity in the business world. Your propensity for brainwaves is a gift: not everyone possesses it, but it is vital to the success of your company (and this is true whether you work for yourself, a small family firm, a large corporation or the public sector).

There is a real shortage of creative people in the business world. According to research carried out in 2005 by Arts & Business (a government-funded organization that helps business people support the arts and the arts inspire business people), 86 per cent of prospective candidates for board-level appointments were seen to lack the creative skills necessary for those positions. Creative skills are highly valued and seen as being one of the key elements of business success. The ability to generate new ideas is built into the job descriptions of four out of five top-level appointments.

And yet, businesses are struggling to find people who can offer these skills. The consultants interviewed by Arts & Business concluded that a lack of suitable training, dull and unexciting work environments and organizational cultures that do not encourage the development of creative skills were largely to blame.[5]

Those businesses that do encourage and promote creativity see the benefits in their results. Software company SAS prides itself on its culture of creativity and has developed a series of policies and ways of working that encourage originality and experimentation. It claims that its low rates of staff turnover (3–5 per cent compared with an industry average of nearly 20 per cent), its 98 per cent software subscription renewal rate and nearly 30 years of revenue growth are all the result of its ability to harness the creative energies of its staff and its customers.[6]

And, if you needed more proof, just ask the trouble-shooter himself, Sir John Harvey Jones. In *Making it Happen – Reflections on Leadership*, he writes at length about the value of dreaming and how he, in his years at ICI, encouraged adventurous thinking and playing with fanciful ideas. His justification?

> 'It has to be possible to dream and speak the unthinkable, for the only thing we do know is that we shall not know what tomorrow's world will be like.'[7]

A company that is not changing is actually going backwards, and a company cannot change unless ideas can be generated about how, why and when the company *should* change. Creative people are needed to provide these ideas – and not just for new products or new services. Ideas are also needed to solve internal problems: how can we attract a more diverse range of employees? How can we retain staff for longer? How can we make it easier for people to take holidays when they want to take them? How can we spend less time in meetings? How can we get more value from the meetings we attend? How can we make visitors to our offices feel more welcome?

You don't need to sit on the board to be able to influence how you and your organization works.

Case study – 'Biddy'

My first job was as a library assistant in a university. When I went there I had an idea that I wanted to meet people in every department. Every time an opportunity came up I said, 'I want to do that.' I got a good reputation in many ways. This was the most junior member of staff doing this, but I got to know senior people beyond the issue desk.

If you didn't say you wanted to do something different you stayed there and I can't imagine anything more boring. I taught myself the Russian alphabet so I could translate Russian titles on exchange books. I stood in at the interlibrary exchange department so I would meet people. I volunteered to work in the under-grad. library so I would meet the students. I wanted different experiences and I used my extrovert nature to talk my way into it.

Your ticket to the top

But if you're so creative and businesses need and value creativity so much, why aren't you more successful?

Well, we already know how you hold yourself back with your short attention span, lack of an eye for detail and habit of leaving projects nearly complete. And, as we've seen in the Arts & Business research, companies want creative people but they don't necessarily have the infrastructure to enable these kinds of employees to shine. Few organizations are built around enabling enterprise, innovation and exploration like SAS.

Face it – you aren't always a safe pair of hands. Combine that with a tendency for companies to be risk-averse and you can see why your route to the top has been littered with obstacles.

But Hyper-Creative people *can* make it to the top. Look at your typical entrepreneurial types: Simon Woodroffe of Yo! Sushi; Tim Smit of The Eden Project; Richard Branson of Virgin... These are people who have the same preferences as you but have found ways to cash in on their enthusiasm, imagination and big ideas. And one of the ways they have done this is by surrounding themselves with the right people – people who fill the gaps, who can turn raw ideas into strategies, who can write financial reports, who can dot 'i's and cross 't's, and who can handle the extremes to which Hyper-Creatives are prone.

We'll find out more about these strange creatures in Chapter Four. But for the moment, let's discover a little more about you.

CHAPTER THREE

I LOVE YOU JUST THE WAY YOU ARE

If you've got this far, you've probably decided that you are a Hyper-Creative. If you are a 'gut feeling' type of Hyper-Creative you probably knew the minute you picked the book off the shelf.

But if you are going to turn your Hyper-Creativity into a secret weapon that gets you to the top, you'll need to know a little more about it and how it differentiates you from everyone else.

JUNG AT HEART

It all started in the 1920s with Carl G. Jung's 1923 book *Psychological Types* [8]. He was looking for a way to categorize the habitual thinking patterns and actions he saw in individuals, in order to better understand and, perhaps, predict how people behave. He broke these habits in to three dimensions of personality:

The first dimension: Related to the source and direction of a person's energy. Are we focused more towards the outer or the inner world? He used the terms 'extraversion' and 'introversion' to distinguish the two preferences.

The second dimension: Related to how we perceive information and the kind of information to which we are attracted. He used the terms 'sensing' for a preference for data that we recognize through our senses, and 'intuition' for a preference for abstract data that we recognize through our intuition.

The third dimension: Related to the way we make decisions or judgements about the information we have received. He differentiated between 'thinking', which involved decision-making based on a cause-and-effect analysis and 'feeling' where decisions are made on the basis of personal values and beliefs.

If you are familiar with the Myers-Briggs Type Indicator, you will recognize these terms. Mother and daughter psychologists Katharine Briggs and Isabel Briggs Myers used Jung's theories to develop a test for personality preferences. In addition to his three dimensions, they added a fourth that focused on a preference for either orderliness and decisiveness ('judgement') or flexibility and freedom ('perception').

There are many different psychological and personality profiling tools, like MBTI, on the market and each uses terminology in a very specific and controlled way to describe how people prefer to operate in the work environment and outside.

I've used some of this terminology in this book and introduced different terms where appropriate.

So, although I use 'extrovert' and 'introvert', I do not use the MBTI terms 'sensing' and 'intuition', 'thinking' and 'feeling', or 'judgement' and 'perception' when describing Hyper-Creatives. This is intentional. My conclusions (while inspired by the work of people like Jung and Myers and Myers-Briggs) are based not on rigorous scientific research but on my own observations, conversations with my clients and my personal thinking around the subject.

I've tried to use more accessible terminology like 'creative' and 'practical', 'analytical' and 'beliefs-driven', and 'structured' and 'flexible'. Even so, whilst you might recognize these terms from other profiling tools, remember that the descriptions of what they mean within the context of Hyper-Creativity are entirely my own. The term creativity will have a range of different meanings. The kind of Hyper-Creativity that I am exploring is rather different from the creativity described by these other psychometric tools.

EXTROVERT OR INTROVERT?

Extroverts use interaction to create the energy they need to get through the day[9]. Talking inspires and helps them adapt their ideas, but their need to talk about everything can be annoying to people around them. In the office there is a time and a place for brainstorming but the rest of the time we are expected to present fully formed ideas. Colleagues are normally working on their own projects. An extrovert's need to discuss his or her work can be distracting to others and, while it may help the extrovert, it doesn't help anyone else at all. In fact, it may make their job even harder.

Where extroverts can really shine is in meetings. Unlike introverts, extroverts will probably look forward to meetings, particularly those that set aside time for discussing options and solving problems. The danger is that extroverts dominate the proceedings and do not acknowledge when the time for exploring is over. Because their ideas come thick and fast and are sparked by what other people contribute, they may not leave introvert people – who prefer to consider their thoughts and order their ideas – time to express themselves.

Extroverts can be impulsive. Because they don't spend a lot of time thinking ideas through, they often rush into making a decision before they have fully considered the implications. Combine this with the high level of enthusiasm that often accompanies the extrovert personality and you could have a loose cannon on your hands if the extrovert does not learn how to manage their personality effectively.

According to authors Mike Southon and Chris West, in their very useful book *The Boardroom Entrepreneur*[10], entrepreneurs are generally extroverts. It is this that helps them see beyond the way that things are now, and imagine how they might be different. Entrepreneurs love a problem. Instead of panicking, they immediately want to figure out how to solve it. Their extroversion also contributes to their charisma and ability to inspire others. They enjoy meeting other people, and so are probably well-networked and endlessly enthusiastic (at least at the start of a project or the inception of an idea). However, their extroversion can mean they are not team players. When other people can't 'keep up', the extrovert entrepreneur is likely to plough ahead, which can be disruptive to the unity of the team.

Not all entrepreneurs are extroverts however. And not all Hyper-Creatives are either.

'Entrepreneurs love a problem. Instead of panicking, they immediately want to figure out how to solve it'

Just because you are an introvert doesn't mean you don't have good ideas. Introverts are just as busy thinking and creating. It's just that it's all going on inside rather than outside for all to see. As an extrovert myself I was rather jealous of introverts when I read Pearman and Albritton's description of what's going on inside their head. They claim that introverts 'draw sustenance from a vivid and rich inner world of thoughts and ideas'.[11]

Introverts are much maligned and it has become commonly accepted that extroverts are preferable in the workplace because extroversion is associated with a confident, outgoing personality. Introverts are thought to be shy and lacking in self-esteem, when actually there is no link between these characteristics. In fact, it is just as common for extroverts to be lacking in confidence. Sometimes the need to talk everything through is really a need to get confirmation that an idea is a good one. And we all know that the person who speaks the loudest is often the one with the least self-assurance.

Introverts like to prepare before they speak. Having spent time alone working on a problem internally, they are able to think through the implications and develop their thoughts. Like extroverts they may change their minds during this process but rather than doing so aloud they do it in their heads.

On the upside, when an introvert gives their opinion it has often been considered thoroughly and at that point is unlikely to change.

On the downside, it may not be clear to others how the introvert came to that conclusion. Just as in a maths exam, sometimes colleagues will want to see your 'workings' in the belief that the way in which you came to your conclusions is as important as the conclusion itself.

'Introverts are able to think through the implications of a problem and develop their thoughts'

Email is perfectly designed for the introvert as it gives a valid excuse not to visit people in person. An extrovert may feel increasingly frustrated and isolated by email communication. The introvert much prefers to communicate in this way – if your boss is an introvert your inbox will probably be full of her missives, while an extrovert boss is more likely to turn up at your desk wanting to be updated face to face.

Introverts also prefer to focus on fewer tasks but in more depth. Juggling is not the introvert's style and coping with a large number of diverse projects will cause her increasing levels of stress. What the extrovert sees as brainstorming, the introvert may hear as an increasingly long list of things to do. And you can see why the introvert, surrounded by brainstorming extroverts, starts to feel at first frustrated and then overwhelmed.

Case study – 'Kat'

My husband is an introvert and I am an extrovert. He thinks I am great. Fantastic. But he can't provide some of what I need. I need someone who I can talk things through with and I don't know why but he can't do that.

He's like a cat. He just sits there looking at you, blinking. We have a very high phone bill because I have to call people who are like me.

You will probably recognize yourself as having elements of both the introvert and the extrovert. Despite being an extrovert myself, I solve many problems while swimming lengths at the local pool or watching TV. In those cases, my introvert side is doing its bit. It isn't always necessary for me to talk about everything in order to know what I think. And even if you are largely introverted, you can probably remember situations where you came up with an idea as you spoke with others.

Case study – 'Mike'

I am an introvert and extrovert in almost exactly equal measure so I have seen the impact of both. When I am at my most introverted, people around me feel they don't get any warning that there is something wrong until it's a crisis. This can mean that I fall over, because there's no one there to support me, because they didn't realize there was a problem, or they fall over because I've suddenly announced that I am going to sell my house and move to Australia and no one saw any of this coming.

My extrovert side doesn't cause so many problems except that I can raise expectations in other people that I am going to do certain things and then they think I have gone slightly mad because next time I see them I have totally changed direction. I was just testing an idea out, gathering reaction. It doesn't mean I am going to do it. But they took my blathering as being a commitment about what I was going to do.

What will really help you manage yourself more effectively is to increase your level of awareness about your thinking style. There are pros and cons to both introversion and extroversion depending on the circumstances, the preferences of your colleagues and the requirements of individual projects. When a decision has to be made in the moment, drawing on your extrovert abilities to quickly run through the options and make your choice is more appropriate than asking if you can go back to your desk and think about it for 48 hours. Recognizing where you do your best introverted thinking (the bath, the supermarket, walking) and where you do your best extroverted thinking (in a meeting you have prepared for, against a deadline, with people you know well) will help you hone your skills.

PRACTICAL OR CREATIVE?

All Hyper-Creatives are creative. The clue is in the title. That isn't to say you cannot also be practical or that all of your ideas set the world alight, but your preference is for original thought.

Creativity is often found to run in families[12]. That doesn't mean creativity is necessarily genetic but simply that particular family environments may encourage creativity of thought and expression. Different types of creativity may manifest themselves in members of the same family. In a family where one member is a writer, it is common to also find artists, musicians, dancers and mathematicians as well as other writers amongst siblings, parents, children and cousins[13].

Because of this, it is hard to say whether your creativity is learnt or innate. Raised in a family where ideas were not discussed and where you had no other outlet to express this preference, you may not have become as creative as you could have been. When you look at the rest of your family, you may not see others like you – perhaps you are something of a rogue in this respect. But maybe your family express their creativity in other ways, or maybe your key influences did not come from the family but from books, television or friends.

In a sense, while it is interesting to ponder (if you like that kind of thing) it doesn't matter. The fact is that these days you are drawn towards creative tasks.

The details aren't really what interest you – you're always looking for the big idea, the grand vision. You don't want your idea to solve a one-off problem, but to prevent problems like that from ever happening again. One idea leads to another idea and anything can spark your imagination – a book, a comment, a flash that seems to come from nowhere. When you are on fire, you are really on fire and will work through the night on your project.

The problem comes, as we've already discovered, with implementation. At this point you get bored. You also have a blind spot for detail, which is one of the reasons some of your revolutionary ideas stumble at the first hurdle – they are missing a vital element that you, in your enthusiasm, overlooked.

'Leaders have more in common with artists than managers in their approach to problem-solving'

Creative people are more comfortable with chaos and lack of structure. In much of the published work on leadership and management, one of the features that is said to differentiate the two is that leaders tend to take a more creative approach to problem-solving and have more in common with artists than managers in the way they operate[14].

Leaders use a creative approach to develop a direction for their team or organization. They are proactive instead of reactive. They anticipate obstacles ahead and may prefer to talk about desires for the future and compelling objectives rather than setting specific, measurable, detailed goals. They also enjoy working with lots of options. While managers try to close down options so that everyone is in agreement, much like mediators or diplomats, leaders like to develop new, fresh approaches and open up new options. They avoid repetitive, mundane tasks and tend to take more risks. There's the safe, tried and tested option and then there's the new, exciting, never-been-attempted option. Guess which one the creative leader is drawn to?

Practical people, by contrast, feel more confident with a standard solution, knowing it has been proven to be effective. Their focus is more short-term – 'What do we need to do now?' – and their preference is for detailed processes where every step clearly follows the last. Effectiveness and efficiency are their buzzwords and repetition does not concern them. In fact, they may enjoy repetition, knowing that they can make incremental improvements one step at a time when they revisit the task.

Practical people can act as a reality check to the creative process – this can be limiting when what is needed is more ideas, but useful when brainstorming is getting out of hand.

Case study – 'Sophie'

I can get into the detail as long as I can see the big picture in my head. Once that's gone I start to think, 'This isn't working'. I have to keep a view of what we are doing and why. Everything has to interlink somehow.

If people start discussing the detail in ridiculous depth when we haven't started anything and we aren't ready for the nitty-gritty, I get very frustrated. I feel we can adapt as we go along if we understand the overall direction.

Remember that your work preferences may be different to your non-work preferences. Sometimes creative people like us can get a great deal of satisfaction from practical tasks outside of work to balance the creativity we use the rest of the time. Sometimes we just want to do something mundane that doesn't involve solving a problem, like the dishes or the ironing.

ANALYTICAL OR BELIEFS-DRIVEN?

Hyper-Creatives can be either analytical or beliefs-driven. If you are extrovert, creative and flexible being analytical offers you a little balance. If you are extrovert, creative, flexible and beliefs-driven then you probably face a number of problems in turning ideas into action.

This is because those of us who make our decisions based on our beliefs tend not to take too much notice of the facts. Or rather, we believe that our gut feeling, our past experience and our values are a more reliable measure of what will work than collecting a lot of data. After all, you can never have *all* of the facts. If you waited until you had collated every piece of information available you would never make a decision. And anyway, is there such a thing as a fact? Isn't all data flawed in some way? Don't the answers you get depend on what questions you ask?

You see what we do? We undermine the validity of research in order to justify not doing any. If you combine that with the traits of an extrovert (love to talk rather than going away and considering their thoughts first) and the traits of the creative (love big ideas, don't care much for detail) you've already got a rather dangerous mix. Throw flexibility in the pot and there is likely to be an explosion!

Beliefs-driven people have a set of values that inform their decisions. They 'just know' that something is right or wrong. These values and beliefs may have developed over the years as a result of experience and can therefore be very reliable. When you've worked in an industry for 30 years, you are in a good position to make quick decisions based on a gut feeling that has been honed over a working career.

In addition, where some decisions are concerned, your gut feeling, or sense of whether or not something is right for you, is the only thing that matters. You can produce a list detailing exactly what you are looking for in your ideal house or life partner or pet but then fall in love with one that doesn't meet any of the criteria. And your list ceases to matter.

Gut-feeling decision-makers evoke awe among less courageous souls. It suggests a level of confidence that we all seek, even if the decisions that are made this way are deeply flawed[15]. And gut feeling is a natural companion to creativity because the generation of breakthrough ideas doesn't usually come from an analysis of the data, but instead from obscure sources of inspiration that can't be traced and documented.

A talent for gut-feeling decision-making is a commodity you can take with you anywhere. Sometimes you can't access the facts. Sometimes there isn't time. Sometimes a decision has to be made quickly (such as in the case of a stockbroker who chooses to buy or sell amidst the mayhem of the trading floor) and people who are comfortable with making snap decisions based on a feeling are hugely valuable.

'Sometimes tough decisions are vital to the success of a business'

Of course, sometimes these decisions are just plain wrong. The city whizz kid who plumps for 'buy, buy, buy' and then sees the market crash may live to regret that decision. He assessed the risk in the blink of an eye and decided to go for it. But was his assessment accurate?

Gut-feeling decision-makers know that from time to time they will be wrong. But they guess that they are wrong as frequently as if they had relied on the data, which can also lead to wrong decisions. They argue that they can live with the mistakes (and learn from them) because they were true to themselves.

Analytical decision-makers try to leave emotion out of the process. At an extreme, they coolly assess the information available and only afterwards consider the implications of their decisions for the feelings of other people. They gather evidence first. They do not make up their mind until they have the data. They are not swayed by rousing speeches nor impassioned arguments. They want to know how much all this is going to cost.

Beliefs-driven people will gather research but, unless they use a great deal of self-restraint, the facts will simply reinforce their argument. They will leave out information that conflicts with their position.

The analytical thinker will have set down decision-making criteria at the start of the research process. He will have a clear objective in mind and stay focused on the job at hand. And, because the data tells him what decision to make, he can often make tougher choices than someone who is motivated by a sense of fairness. As we know, sometimes such tough decisions are vital to the success of a business.

Case study – 'Biddy'

My husband and I laugh about this. There is 'right' and there is 'Biddy's right'. In the family I am known as HW – hard work. That's because I am so determined that I am right. We make a joke about how many times John is allowed to be right. When we are in the car I say, 'I am sure we go this way', and my husband says, 'No, we go this way', but I insist that my instincts are right. The problem is that John is a geographer and has a better sense of direction than me. But I'm still right. I just know it!

STRUCTURED OR FLEXIBLE?

Just take a look at your desk. Compare it to the desks of those around you. Do you have a system for keeping important documents? Can you find what you need? Are you consistently early, on time or late for meetings? Do you know what you have to do today?

Some people just love lists – they like to tick boxes when everything is complete. At the end of the day they clear their desk of papers, take their empty coffee cup to the sink and make sure all their drawers are closed. All old paperwork that is no longer needed is binned or shredded. They have less than 20 emails in their inbox, all of which have been opened and read. They can find a pen when they need one. They may even have a name label on their hole-punch.

Other people are always having last minute disasters. The train always breaks down, the traffic is always a nightmare and their phone is always out of battery. The word 'deadline' has a unique meaning to them, simply indicating the date at which they will ask for their first extension. They will need to sift through two or three piles of paper to find the document they need. They always have to borrow someone else's pen. And they never use a hole-punch because they never file anything.

These are extremes of course but even if we think we are more balanced than this we probably know people who all but conform to these descriptions.

And it would be natural to assume that structured is better than flexible. Surely the list-keepers and schedule-makers are more valuable in a work environment? Well, they are certainly easier to manage on a day-to-day basis. They enjoy clear goals and objectives and manage their time so that they usually get their work done. This means they are reliable and their progress towards their targets can be easily monitored. As effectiveness in the workplace is often judged by these criteria, a structured employee is highly desirable.

On the other hand, they can get stressed, and under stress their attention to detail and their ability to focus are disrupted. When chaos breaks out, as it sometimes does, they find it hard to cope. When the goal changes halfway through a project, or an unpredicted piece of information means that it's back to the drawing board, they can become frustrated. They also expect everyone to be like this and cannot understand their flexible colleagues. They may want everything to just return to normal so they can get back on track and will find it very challenging when other people seem to relish disorder and uncertainty.

The flexibles have their burdens to bear of course. They like to gather information and ideas and will postpone action until they think they have enough. While the structured employee is already on step three, the flexible employee is still researching. My dad always says, 'Tidy desk, tidy mind', and, in the case of flexible people, the implications of this comment are true too: their desks are untidy, their minds a mess of diverse information lying in haphazard piles.

But flexible people adapt much better than their structured friends to change. Sometimes a problem is ambiguous and needs a more laid-back, hands-off approach until a way forward emerges. At times where the future is unknown or when a matter is outside their 'circle of influence' (more on this later), a flexible person will be perfectly at home. The structured person will be a quivering wreck trying to take control of issues that, quite frankly, cannot be controlled.

And sometimes it is genuinely more important to move the deadline and complete the research or brainstorming than to make a snap decision in order to hit your target and regret it at your leisure.

Case study – 'Miranda'

I am actually quite structured but I wish I was more flexible. I associate structure with being rigid. I can dig my heels in a bit. Sometimes it wouldn't matter, there are different ways of doing things, many ways to skin a cat, whereas I say, 'These are the steps you have to take.'

I associate flexibility with relaxation, whereas structure is associated with tension.

Being structured doesn't mean I like detail – I always have a few projects on the go at once because I get bored easily. At the moment I have three piles of projects I am working on in my office. The piles are really tidy but I have to force myself to do things. The thing that forces me is a deadline. I never miss the deadline but I do work right up to the last minute.

I think this works quite well – the person I am doing the project for will never know the last minute nature of the end product and from my perspective it is all fresh in my mind, which is good for me.

Right, that's enough about you. You know what you are like. I know what you are like. But of course, not everyone else is like us. That can cause problems, as I am sure you know by now. But it's also fortunate because, without the Non-Hyper-Creatives, we'd be all talk and no trousers.

CHAPTER FOUR

YOU ARE NOT ALONE

Just like the mayfly, 'action' has a life cycle. It starts with the formation of a creative idea, where two or more previously unrelated thoughts interlock, resulting in a leap of imagination. This is the *Eureka!* moment that occurs at 3am or while you're swimming laps or, if you're lucky, in the dying seconds of a brainstorming session. (I say 'If you're lucky'... in my experience of facilitating such events, brilliant ideas tend not to occur at the very start of a brainstorming session, or even halfway through; just like a lost umbrella, brilliant ideas tend to be in the last place you thought of looking.)

But a raw idea is like a newborn baby – it can't survive for long on its own. So next comes the development stage, honing the idea into a workable strategy, ironing out the kinks, finding the resources and the people needed to move the idea forward.

So far though, nothing has actually happened. Nothing has changed. The next step is setting some goals – what has to be done and by when – in order for action to occur. And now we start seeing activity. The idea is no longer a vague concept or even a plan. It's happening. Results can be seen.

And it's still not the end of the process, because now it needs refining, tweaking, updating. Standards need to be maintained and then improved. And perhaps some of the shortcomings of the idea in action come to light. These shortcomings, problems that need to be solved, feed the creative juices and, with any luck, create new *Eurekas!* at 3am. And so the cycle continues.

Left to our own devices, we Hyper-Creatives will get stuck at stage one (the ideas phase), perhaps dipping our toes into the waters of stage two (the development phase), only to discover that it's a bit chilly for our tastes, then reverting to a nice warm spot in the sun where we can go back to thinking exciting new thoughts.

In order to turn ideas into action we need other people to complete the cycle. Even if you are sufficiently motivated to address your weaknesses and determined to follow through to completion by using the strategies in this book, there will be times when your own sheer determination is not enough to overcome your natural preferences.

Besides, constantly working against those natural preferences is hard work, and why should you work so hard? You already have a gift for creativity. Your time is better spent honing these skills than struggling to master a set of skills that will never be a good fit for you.

Of course, there are times when you will have to, or want to, see a project through from beginning to end. But even in those cases, trying to do so alone will be stressful for you. The right combination of people around you to support, encourage, assist and contribute will help relieve some of this stress and make the whole process far more enjoyable and fulfilling.

In addition, by now you have a list of incompletions cluttering your brain. Every time you start a new endeavour there will be a voice in your head that reminds you how rarely you actually finish anything (providing countless examples to prove the point). As if your natural disinclination to finish what you start were not enough, this 'negative self-talk', which we will return to at a later stage, will compound the problem. You are not starting with a clean slate.

Therefore, any chance you get to change this pattern, using the support of other people, will help you provide counter-evidence to this undermining, distrustful voice of doom. You'll have evidence that your ideas do come to fruition and increasingly the fact that you can, and do, finish what you start will overshadow the presence of those instances when you did not. In this way you start to build a track record that not only convinces other people that you have changed, but (more importantly) convinces *you*.

The first resource you are going to need to turn your ideas into results is a support team. This group of people can fill the gaps in your personality, meaning the whole action lifecycle is covered. But if we leave creating this support team to chance we are likely to miss some core elements. And not everyone understands Hyper-Creatives. Unless you select your team with care you may find you have a resource that doesn't actually work for you.

> **'A support team can fill the gaps in your personality'**

THE SUCCESS SQUAD – WHAT IT IS NOT

Many of us work in teams. Most of us don't get to choose the members of our team. We have colleagues we must work alongside, who do the same job as us or a complimentary job, and who may be senior or junior to us.

Even if you are self-employed you may still find yourself working in an informal team made up of other freelancers, clients, customers, suppliers or administrative staff. Some of these you work with by choice. Others you work with out of necessity and you make the best of the fact that it isn't always a match made in heaven.

In this chapter we are going to look at how to put together a 'Success Squad' of individuals who will support you in turning your ideas into action and results. The Success Squad exists in addition to the team you already work with. Some members of your Success Squad may be colleagues. But equally members may be drawn from your wider circle – family, friends and individuals you know professionally but do not work alongside.

Why is this? Well, firstly because sacking or replacing all the people you work with at the moment may not be within your authority. Unless you are in a position within your company that allows you to fire anyone at will and rebuild a team from scratch, you'll have to learn to work with what you've got. And even if you are in a position to do this, think twice. You don't want to find yourself in the running for the 'Worst Boss in the World' award.

Secondly, you don't require the Success Squad full-time. They are a resource you can call on to help you harness your creative powers. When you don't need them they can get on with their lives.

THE SUCCESS SQUAD – WHAT IT IS

The purpose of the Success Squad is to help you minimize the negatives of being Hyper-Creative while maximizing the benefits. Success Squad members need never meet one another. And there are distinct advantages to having some members of this unit outside your day-to-day team.

As an example, you may want a creative thinking partner – someone who is also highly creative who brainstorms with you, contributes ideas and helps you to develop your own. One of your direct reports may not feel completely at ease in this role with you, their boss. Equally, you may not want a peer at work to perform this role for political reasons. And your own boss may not be suitable as she may want you to come to her not with ideas but with solutions.

In my case, my Success Squad is made up of my business coach, my business manager, my PA, my bookkeeper, about four or five friends and colleagues and my partner. Between us we cover the whole lifecycle of an action because, to be frank, nothing much would ever get done if I tried to handle all the stages myself.

Because the role my friends and my partner play in this team is informal, I provide a reciprocal arrangement. When any of them want to tap into my creative abilities I am glad to oblige.

Not everyone I know, like or work with is a Success Squad member. Not everyone wants to talk about my ideas. Not everyone can help me develop them in a way that really helps me make them work. And, often, it isn't actually appropriate for me to ask certain colleagues, clients, even some friends, to perform this role for me.

Extrovert Hyper-Creatives in particular find it hard to talk about much else when they are working on a great idea. Their idea becomes their obsession and they will tell everyone and anyone about it. Learning some self-control and identifying who the right people are to mull your thoughts over with will prevent you becoming a drain on those friends and colleagues who enjoy your company for reasons other than your creativity.

And, in case you introvert Hyper-Creatives think you can do without the Success Squad, think again. Unless you bring other people into your circle, it is likely that no one will know you even had an idea, let alone assist you in turning it into something tangible.

There are three key considerations when putting together the right team of people to help you make the most of your gift and minimize its limitations:

- Innate work-style preference.
- Right work, right person.
- Attitude.

INNATE WORK STYLE PREFERENCE

Just as your success relies on focusing as much as possible on those activities you are innately suited to, members of your Success Squad should be chosen because they have innate preferences that compliment your own.

Ideally you will have at least one of each of the following in your Squad:

Creative Thinking Partner

No surprises here. You need people around you who understand how creative thinking works. Stand-up comics know that not everything they say will be funny. But if they thought about it too much before they opened their mouths they would lose the moment. So they say what pops in to their mind and although some one-liners will fall flat, most of them will get a laugh.

Other creative people understand that the same is true with the imagination. Even those with a different combination of preferences to you will know how to support you in developing your ideas. They understand that not every idea you have will fly but they don't interrupt your flow because the next idea you fire out could be gold. And they won't knock your ideas down because they know, at this stage, that what you need to do is explore. They

'Hyper-Creatives generally get bored at about the time when a project becomes too detailed'

will help you build on your imagination by getting excited, having their own ideas to feed into your thought process and letting you experiment with your ideas, no matter how unrealistic or fantastic they become.

Later in this book we'll look more at brainstorming and how to really flex your creative muscles. You may want the Creative Thinking Partner in your Success Squad to read that chapter too so they can help you even more!

Detail Demon

Hyper-Creatives generally get bored at about the time when a project becomes too detailed. Fact-finding, double-checking data, proof-reading, financial matters... all these can be a huge strain. And yet without detail your plans are likely to remain on the drawing board.

Detail Demons can see the flaws in an idea. They are interested in whether it will work and how it will work. Their preference is for facts and data and they are generally extrovert. When you tell them your great idea they are full of questions: Has someone else already thought of it? How much would it cost? Is there time? Are there any loop-holes in the concept?

They may not actually do your research for you but running your ideas past a Detail Demon is a vital part of the development process.

Organization Wizard

If your preference is for flexibility you are probably pretty disorganized. While flexibility helps you to be innovative, comfortable with risk and free to explore, it may also mean you can never find your car keys and you always pay your bills on the final red demand.

The Organization Wizard in your Success Squad is the one who arranges your direct debit and gets you a key chain that beeps when you whistle. They will invent a system that supports you in getting to appointments and paying suppliers on time. They may take your calls, manage your diary or book your taxis. They may look after your database and remind you to sign your tax return two weeks before it is due.

Their preference is for structure and data and this person could even double up as your Detail Demon. However the best way to use their talent is not by running ideas past them but asking them to solve problems and make changes. They prefer to be hands-on. They will actually do jobs for you as far as they can (short of forging your signature... although, if you ask nicely...).

Delivery Guy

Once your idea is ready for implementation, you may not be the most suitable person for the job. You might want to be involved at the start while the project is being tweaked and refined but once it comes to daily delivery you are likely to get bored and stressed. And getting too involved with the day-to-day workings of a new business or a project will take you away from being creative.

However, some people love the delivery far more than developing the original ideas. Give them a job to do and they will get on and do it. They'll do it day after day, rarely getting tired of it so long as they find the subject matter interesting.

These people are primarily practical in their innate preferences. You'll recognize them because they are the ones who just want to get started. They can't wait for you creative types to do your bit so they can get on and do the work.

Quality Controller

Because you tend to be hands-off you don't always know what is happening on the ground. Your enthusiastic Delivery Guy might not be carrying out his part with precision. Or the idea may be getting out of date and need upgrading. Or complaints may be gathering but no one is taking action.

A Quality Controller will know what to look for and what questions to ask to ensure your idea is being implemented and updated in a way that really respects all the hard work that went into creating it. An eye for detail is important here as is a good gut feeling. Quality Controllers will often have a preference for introversion while also being practical. They may be beliefs-driven or analytical but generally have a good eye for spotting the moment when standards are starting to slip. While you are off being creative, this guy is keeping an eye on things on the ground and feeding back to you.

Coach

Coaches come in all shapes and sizes. Some are creative, others practical, others analytical and others beliefs-driven.

But what they have is an ability to get you to think more deeply without really sharing their own thoughts and ideas. A Coach isn't like your Creative Thinking Partner who winds you up into a frenzy of excitement. The Coach is more detached – enthusiastic but objective. He may not have answers like the Organization Wizard, or see holes like the Detail Demon, but will guide you by asking questions and assisting you in finding the answers yourself.

Time with the Coach is time to be calm, to take a step back and get some perspective. The Coach in your Success Squad need not be a professional full-time Executive Coach. And, depending on their personal style and their ability to listen, your Creative Thinking Partner or your Detail Demon may be able to flex their style in order to adopt this role. But ensuring you have someone or more than one person in your Squad who asks you questions and lets you think is crucial.

Case study – 'Tony'

In terms of creating what you describe as a Success Squad, I am getting there. I have two business partners who are a big help to me. They are similar in many ways to me but they have made a profitable business, which gives me a lot of courage, if you like. There's another chap I know who I used to work with who would make an excellent project manager. I really admire him and hope eventually to have him in my business. He does like to get into the detail of things. He doesn't have the overall picture like I do but it's like you need the sales person, your general manager and your ideas person. And he would be great as the general manager.

I am the ideas person. I don't have any 'big man' requirement to be the boss, but I do have a certain sense that I have to be the leader, and let other people get on with the practical side just because I need to have autonomy and when you are the leader you get that.

About a year ago I had a major wake up call. This guy, the project manager, said, 'Have you any idea how creative you are?' And I said 'No, I haven't'. I hadn't realized I had something special to offer because it came so naturally to me. It was him who said I had to do something that I had my heart in. And that's why I set up the business. That was the catalyst.

RIGHT WORK, RIGHT PERSON

I used to have a PA who was bad at organization. Lovely girl but always losing bits of paperwork.

In making your Success Squad work you need to ensure that the right people are doing the right work for them in the right way for them. This is your responsibility because it's your team. You may not be the boss at work and in the 'real world' you may not be senior to all the people in your Success Squad, but you have selected these individuals to be part of your formal or informal support team and you need to manage them.

That means respecting their areas of preference. I once arranged a brainstorming meeting for my whole Success Squad to talk about the future of my business. Two days before it was due to happen there were some transport problems in London and getting to the meeting was going to be more challenging than normal for a lot of the team.

But it wasn't those furthest away who were most concerned about the travel arrangements and keen to postpone. It was those who do not get their buzz from generating ideas in a meeting-type forum. Although all of them perform a vital function for me personally and professionally, a day of brainstorming was not hugely appealing and when an obstacle got in the way they realized how weak their motivation was to attend.

I admit I was frustrated. I had been looking forward to the meeting and done a fair amount of preparation. Instead, with the spare time I had, I met with one of the people in my Squad who had ideas and a head for business. In two hours I had a clear way forward and decided not to consult anyone else on the concept, only on the practicality.

ATTITUDE

Even if you find people who fit all the criteria for a Success Squad member and identify roles they can play that fit neatly with their preferences, there's one more vital element if the team is going to function.

The final piece in creating your Success Squad is ensuring that everyone has the right attitude. As I said right at the start of this chapter, not everyone gets Hyper-Creative people. Some try to change us. Others find us annoying (strange but true!). Still others think we are brilliant creative minds but they have no idea how to help us.

Put two Organization Wizards next to each other and one will find you high-maintenance while the other finds you an exciting challenge. Identifying your boundaries will help you select which Organization Wizard or which Detail Demon is right for you.

By 'boundaries' I mean the rules you have about the way other people may behave around you. For instance, I have a boundary whereby other people can criticize the idea but not criticize me. Although in life I will experience personal criticism, I do not want members of my Success Squad to breach this boundary. So in addition to having complimentary personal preferences, I also want them to like me and accept me as a person even if they think my ideas are rubbish!

'The Success Squad is all about tapping into the true potential of your ideas'

Another boundary is around interruption. At times when I am 'creating' I prefer to be able to talk without interruption. While we may agree a deadline for this part of the process (e.g. 10 minutes) at which point I will stop and renegotiate or listen to feedback from the other person, during that time I want ideas to flow freely so I can see where they lead me. Everyone in my Success Squad needs to be comfortable with that.

It might sound harsh but there are three factors to remember:

1. The Success Squad is all about tapping into the true potential of your ideas. Anything that inhibits this limits the effectiveness of the team. You have put up with an ineffective method of managing your creative processes all your life. If you are going to create a Success Squad and improve the way you manage your ideas you might as well do it properly.
2. I have not, in the main, had to spell out these boundaries to my Squad. I have selected these particular people because they naturally subscribe to these boundaries themselves. Although some communication, clarification and education is needed from time to time, my Squad are inherently drawn towards this way of working with other people. The same should be true of those you invite into yours.

3. This is a two-way process. Your boundaries must be respected but so must the boundaries of your Squad members. If you have said you need 10 minutes to speak unhindered you must also be willing to listen to others for the length of time they have specified. You will be bringing together like-minded people who have a variety of working styles. You need to respect that if the group is to function effectively.

This final point must be remembered if the Success Squad you create is to stand the test of time. Sometimes Success Squad members will be paid to perform this function in relation to you – they may work on your team or in your organization or for your supplier or customer. Working with you is part of their job.

However, as I have already noted, this will not always be true. A Success Squad member may be a friend or family member or a colleague whose job description does not involve helping you out. While they may genuinely enjoy the jobs you hate, they aren't obliged to support you in this way. Respecting their boundaries, time constraints, mood and, of course, their preferred communication and working style will help you sustain these relationships. Providing a reciprocal arrangement will ensure no one feels used or taken for granted.

You may not be able to pull together a complete Success Squad overnight. You certainly do not want to compromise on its membership given how important getting it right is to your future happiness, prosperity and health. But by looking at who you turn to currently for support and analyzing the effectiveness of that relationship, you can start to make changes straight away.

Of course, even when you've created the perfect Success Squad you will still have one difficult person to deal with and this is someone you just can't get away from – yourself. Let's talk a little about him – or her – in the next chapter.

CHAPTER FIVE

THE DEVIL (AND THE ANGEL) ON YOUR SHOULDER

We all have at least two voices vying for position in our heads at all times. This doesn't mean we're in need of psychiatric care. It's just a fact of life.

One of those voices is very articulate. He is also undermining, critical of you, hugely cautious or highly risk-taking, egotistical, under-confident and distrusting of others. If you don't recognize him by that description maybe this will help:

He's the one who says your ideas probably won't work anyway. He tells you that someone else is probably better at this than you. He reminds you how often you've failed to follow through before and asks, 'Why would this time be any different?' He implies that if you don't do X by the time you are 30 or 40 or 50 you might as well forget it.

The other voice is much less noisy. She sits there quietly while that nasty little devil distracts you. And in a quiet whisper she's the one who remembers that time when you were really committed to a project and you finished it way ahead of schedule. And she nudges you and asks, 'Why shouldn't you be the one to do this?' And she tells you it is never too late to turn your ideas from fantasy into reality.

Don't worry, though, you aren't going nuts. Or, rather, you might be but this isn't the evidence that proves it! We all have these voices.

They form the internal dialogue that helps us make sense of our lives, of what is happening to us, and how we feel about those events.

The bad news is that these voices are making decisions on your behalf. They are guiding your thought processes, impacting your mood and directly affecting your success. What's worse is that now I've told you about them, what was once a vague awareness that they existed will become an annoying distraction, just like when you have a song in your head that you just can't seem to get rid of (normally something extremely naff like 'The Hills are Alive With the Sound of Music' or 'Puppet on a String' – sorry, you will be singing one of those all day now).

The good news is that these voices perform a rather useful function if you can read between the lines, take control of them and even learn to switch them off when it serves you best.

A former coach of mine used to refer to the negative internal voice as my mean Sergeant Major so let's look at him first.

ABOUT SERGEANT MAJOR BARKER

''TEN-SHUN! Call yourselves soldiers? You're a bunch of good-fer-nothing babies. You'll never survive in battle. You're weak, lily-livered, poor excuses fer men. I've seen some sorry sights in my time but even I've never seen such a sorry sight as you. Even your mothers are embarrassed...'

Sergeant Major Barker believes that the way to turn his raw recruits into a fighting force is to push them hard, to bully them, to humiliate them, to test their spirit and toughen them up. Along the way some may drop out but those with the right stuff will find a strength within themselves that they didn't know they had.

Even outside of the military, this kind of attitude is prevalent. The PE teacher at school shouts, 'Come on you lot. Stop dawdling. Put your back into it!' in an effort to spur his class on in the cross-country. Parents make comparisons with other children by pointing out how well Billy always does and asking why you can't be more like him. And children challenge each other with taunts like 'Chicken!' and 'Scaredy-cat' in the hope of getting a reaction.

Inevitably such attitudes make their way into the subconscious. We learn that the stick motivates more than the carrot. Praise is hard to come by and although it feels great when we receive it we believe that such recognition and acknowledgement is only appropriate for extra special effort. And, besides, one should always respond to praise with discomfort, bashfulness and, ideally, rejection. Something like 'Oh, it was nothing' or 'I just got lucky' is about right.

We learn early on to speak to ourselves the way others speak to us. We start to doubt ourselves, to be self-critical, to focus on what we did badly rather than what we did well. For we believe that this is the way to improve ourselves. After all, how can we get better if we don't focus on what we did wrong?

The problem arises when that critical voice dominates and warps your experiences. When someone says, 'Well done!' and the voice says, 'Phew. I got away with it this time, but will I be able to convince them next time that I'm not a total idiot?' you know the voice has gone too far.

This voice, which I think of as Sergeant Major Barker, which Susan Jeffers calls 'The Chatterbox'[16] , and which is often referred to in therapeutic circles as the 'top dog', is attempting to perform a valuable function.

Firstly, he is trying to keep your feet on the ground. Modesty is valued in our society and there is a general dislike of people being too big for their boots. As a child, your developing emotional intelligence told you that, in order to fit in, you too must be self-critical and understated. You made this decision at a young age and it still dominates many of your choices about how to react in public. So, when you come up with your fifth great idea during a brainstorming session, your Sergeant Major voice chips in and tells you to keep your mouth shut. The voice may not be right, but he's trying to protect you.

Secondly, the Sergeant Major's barks are intended to keep you safe. When he proclaims, 'You're not ready to get back on to the singles' scene. You'll have to go to the gym first and get back on that diet!', he's giving you a valid excuse for avoiding something that frightens you. Although it doesn't sound like it, he's actually worried that you will get hurt. Far better to hurt yourself by blaming your single status on being out of shape than risk being hurt by someone else.

So, when you start to put meat on the bones of your latest inventive idea, the Sergeant Major reminds you, 'This is bound to be a damp squib just like all the other ideas you've ever had. It'll never make it off the drawing board.' Just as above, he believes it's far better to stop now than face rejection later on.

Thirdly, in among his unfounded criticisms, there are some good points that are worth considering before you reject them. For example, the Sergeant Major says, 'You've never finished a project like this before. What's going to be different now?' You can either agree and admit defeat before you've even begun or answer the question, 'What is different this time?' Well, this time I have a Success Squad, I have a deadline and I understand my pattern better so I can predict where I am likely to struggle and plan how I will overcome those obstacles.

In this way, the Sergeant Major is rather like a devil's advocate, encouraging you to consider factors you had not considered before and overcome obstacles that lie ahead. But, without treatment, the Sergeant Major can seriously get in the way of your success.

Case study – 'Mike'

I have moments where the nice, calm voice rules and I will do a plan. And then I come back to it and throw it all in the air when the other voice is taking control.

I haven't really learnt to ignore the critical voice. I have to create structures around me that mean that I have to follow through despite all the noise that the chatterbox voice is making. So I might go very public with an idea so I am forced to finish what I started because I don't want to be seen to bottle out. I might go into debt so that I just can't fail – I have to make the idea a success or I will lose everything. This doesn't always work because it means I have sleepless nights thinking, 'Will we be able to pay the bills?'

In order to take control and use Sergeant Major Barker's comments for good rather than bad, you need to understand how he tricks you into listening to him and taking his views seriously.

He presents negative assumptions as fact.

For instance, he'll tell you that no one likes a clever clogs, that you are a clever clogs and that being a clever clogs is 'bad'. Well, that's rather a lot of assumptions, isn't it?

But are they unquestionably true? Perhaps some people do like a clever clogs. Perhaps you aren't one anyway – does having ideas make you a 'clever clogs'? Is there actually anything wrong in being good at something... or being better at something than other people? The implication is that 'clever clogs' is a term of derision. But who says? Maybe it's the clever clogs who get ahead in this world? Maybe they are valued and needed in your company? Maybe you don't even care what people think – you are a clever clogs and you want to embrace it. No one can tell you that that is wrong.

Every time you deconstruct these assumptions you give him less material to work with. Eventually he won't be able to seduce you into believing what he says because you have become adept at identifying the assumptions and blowing them out of the water.

He recalls evidence to support his arguments and conveniently makes you forget the evidence that undermines his arguments.

Just like a great politician, he selectively chooses facts that seem irrefutable. But, just like the assumptions, once you get used to spotting these you can call them into question. One way to identify them is to look for sweeping generalizations: 'Everyone is bored by your ideas'; 'You always start well but you never finish'; 'No one will buy this'.

Also, listen out for evidence that goes back many years: 'Remember when you were 10 and you said you were going to build a castle out of matchsticks and you never finished it? Well, you're still like that today.'

Counter this by spending time considering examples that prove the opposite: the time you were 17 and cycled from coast to coast to raise money for charity. Or the time you wrote that great essay at college. Or the time you helped the team achieve their targets by keeping them focused on the goal.

Keeping mementoes that remind you of your successes will give you a bank of memories to draw on. Your Sergeant Major may only remember the times you failed to follow through, but you'll remember all the times you went above and beyond what was expected.

He distracts you from the real issues and draws your attention to minor issues.

When the Sergeant Major blames your disappointing results on lack of decent time management skills, an inability to prioritize or plain laziness, you may think he is helping you. After all, he's providing you with a list of inadequacies that you could resolve. You could go on a time management course, learn prioritization skills, drink energy drinks, keep an appointments diary – all practical ways to address your weaknesses. So why haven't you done anything about it yet? Because these aren't the real issues!

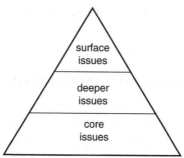

The diagram above shows three levels of issue.

The **Surface Issues** are what we experience as the 'presenting' issue:

Problem: You are always late for work.
Analysis/Solution: You have a problem with time keeping, so get a watch, go on a time management course or get permission to start work later.

The **Deeper Issues** are also sometimes recognized:

> Problem: You are always late for work.
> Analysis/Solution: You don't enjoy work enough because you don't get on with your boss, so learn better communication skills or resign.

But the **Core Issues** are where long term understanding and resolution lie:

> Problem: You are always late for work.
> Analysis/Solution: Your work is not a good fit for your work-style preferences, so renegotiate your role to include more of your preferences, work closely with others with complimentary preferences or look for a new job that more closely fits your style.

Sergeant Major Barker is a simple man. He sees the presenting issue and wants you to resolve that. But unless you deal with the core issue you will continue to be late no matter how many alarm clocks you purchase.

'TALK TO THE HAND' AND OTHER USEFUL TIPS...

So, now you know he's there, what are you going to do about it? We've already touched on some practical strategies such as keeping mementoes of your successes to counter his evidence that you *always* fail, and noticing assumptions and generalizations. But there are basically three ways you can engage with the Sergeant Major when he appears on your shoulder demanding your attention:

Talk to the hand

You don't have to listen to him. Telling him you aren't interested, haven't the time, are otherwise engaged or simply bored of his waffling and using the popular phrase 'Talk to the hand cos the face ain't listening!' often works as a strategy to send him back to where he came from.

Although I have been referring to him as a separate entity, he is, of course, part of you. And for that reason you can switch him off. Something like 'Talk to the hand' works well because it is so dismissive, light-hearted and simple that it doesn't give him further ammunition. It also reminds you that you don't have to take him too seriously.

There are times when engaging him in conversation and listening intently to his repetitive cautions is not worth your valuable time. Send him away (send him off to the Maldives or Hawaii if you think he'd like it there). Give him a vacation and focus on getting on with the job. Practice makes perfect here, so next time you hear his bark, tell him to bog off and see what happens.

Reassure him

Remember that fundamentally he is scared for you. Sometimes he sounds more like a frightened child than an intimidating military man. And that is often when his fear dates from – your childhood. He is expressing the simplistic, childlike, inexperienced fears that you may have had in the past. When you were a child, the taunts of other children were very distressing. It wasn't worth speaking up in class when you had an idea because the risk of being shot down, laughed at or even bullied by other children was too great.

I remember when I was a 30-year-old journalist with nearly a decade's experience of working in the news behind me, being invited to a press conference at Number 11 Downing Street, the home of the Chancellor of the Exchequer. I did my job, interviewed various cabinet ministers and chatted knowledgably to other reporters. When I got outside afterwards I immediately phoned my mother. 'It was amazing,' I proclaimed. 'No one even noticed I was only 12 years old.' My Sergeant Major was still a child and through-out the experience I had to battle with him so I could get my story and not feel like a schoolgirl in disguise.

Had I known then what I know now, I would have told my Sergeant Major that everything was okay, that I would take care of it and that I had enough experience to handle this situation. Visualizing myself stroking his head and repeating, 'There, there,' often helps too.

Engage him in debate

Your third option is to engage with Sergeant Major Barker. Instead of having him in your peripheral awareness, drag him to the front of your mind and ask him to explain himself. What is he saying? What is he worried about? What points is he making?

Now address them. Make a note of all his assumptions, his generalizations and his concerns. Write them down if it helps. A list may suit the more structured of you, a 'brain dump' or stream-of-consciousness may be more suitable for flexible thinkers. Once you have captured all his points, brainstorm your counter arguments.

For instance, let's say you've had an idea but it isn't going to sit well with one or two of your colleagues. Your Sergeant Major may tell you that you'll never convince them, that you are probably wrong anyway and that it's better to keep quiet.

'You'll never convince them' is a sweeping generalization. Ask yourself, 'How would I convince them? How easy would it be to convince them? How long will I give myself to convince them? Do I even need to convince them?' and any other relevant questions. You get to choose how you address this challenge – you don't have to accept Barker's assessment.

'You are probably wrong anyway' can be looked at in the same way. What brought you to this conclusion? What does your research/experience/gut feeling tell you? How reliable are these usually? Are you normally wrong about this stuff? What happened last time or the time before that? And so what if you are wrong? Isn't it valuable to say what you think and learn from your mistakes?

'It's better to keep quiet' is another generalization based on an assumption. Why is it better? Who says? What if it is better to speak up? What do I have to lose? What do I have to gain? Is there any preparation I can do so that speaking up is less risky?

At the end of this process you may still choose not to speak out at this time. But that decision will be based on an assessment of the real risks, the real facts and an adult appraisal of the circumstances rather than a fearful, childish, unfounded response.

Case study – 'Miranda'

I often hear voices which affect my state, and they are more often negative than positive. But I have learnt to ask myself questions in order to shut them up. 'What would I need to believe other people think of me to feel what I am feeling? I would need to believe that they think I'm not very good. Is that true? No. Okay, so move on.'

The critical voice can be so damaging that I have to have a cut-off switch and asking these questions has that effect. I haven't always been able to do this. The penny didn't drop until about three years ago that everything starts with your beliefs and thoughts. It's about managing those.

YOUR OTHER VOICE – THE WISE ONE

I said at the start of this chapter that there were two voices in your head. So far we've only looked at the negative one – Sergeant Major Barker. But what about the angelic little creature on your other shoulder? What's she up to?

Susan Jeffers thinks of this voice as your Higher Self. She describes it as 'self-affirming, loving, giving and abundant'[17]. The problem is that your conscious mind has become so used to listening to the Sergeant Major that it has forgotten that the Higher Self is there and has something very valuable to add.

The Higher Self believes in possibilities, solving problems, even miracles. Your creativity might be inspired by this wise voice. It's the one that asks, 'Why does it need to be this way? Couldn't it be better? How could I make it better?'

The Higher Self also seems to have the power to change your experience of life. If you wake up in a great mood one day, you'll notice how from then on things seem to go rather well. Someone gives you their seat on the train, someone throws in an extra cookie when you buy your latte and you get a phone call confirming you won the contract you were going for. Is this really just a coincidence?

Perhaps. There are many explanations for these results and, depending how spiritual you are, you will choose the one that fits you best. It could be simply that when we are feeling positive we notice positive things. These happen anyway but we overlook them because we are programmed to notice what's wrong rather than what is right.

'The more you listen to your Wise Voice, the louder and stronger she will become'

Alternatively, it could be argued that when you are in such a frame of mind, you put out an energy that others pick up on and reward you for. You smiled at the guy on the train so he gave up his seat. You made the girl behind the counter at the coffee shop laugh so she threw in an extra double choc chip. You could even say that some greater force (God, angels, spirits, karmic energy) makes miracles happen when you tap into your Higher Self.

It doesn't matter. What matters is that we know that good things seem to happen when we are in a good mood. And your good mood, your positive outlook, your 'anything is possible' frame of mind is your Higher Self or your Wise Voice talking.

Because the Wise Voice is a little neglected, it doesn't demand the same attention as the Sergeant Major. It feels like the Sergeant Major is shouting while the Wise Voice is whispering. Sometimes she's the faintest feeling of discomfort or excitement in your gut. Sometimes she's a quiet voice in the back of your head that says, 'You can do this'. And, unlike the Sergeant Major, this voice is encouraging, positive and enthusiastic about you and what you are capable of achieving.

Learning to listen to your intuitive Wise Voice is also a powerful tool against the Sergeant Major. The more you listen to her, give her credit and act on her advice, the louder and stronger she will become.

Try this – next time you think of someone you haven't spoken to for a long time, give them a call. Very often they will say, 'Weird – I was just thinking about you!' or 'How lucky you called. There's something you might be able to help with,' or 'Gosh – I was just looking for an excuse to take 15 minutes break and now I have a valid reason.' What would happen if you trusted this feeling more often?

Just as you sometimes want to capture what that Sergeant Major says so that you can address his concerns, you may also want to capture what the Wise Voice says through writing a list of her comments or brain-dumping. Sometimes the way forward becomes obvious when you listen to this voice and ignore the pointless fears of the Sergeant Major altogether.

I'm afraid that, now you've read about these two little friends inside your head, you are going to become super-aware of their existence. I'm sorry about that… in a way. But seeing as you can't unlearn what you've already learnt, you might as well make the best of it, start getting used to their strange foibles and experimenting with how you can use them to your benefit.

HYPER-CREATIVES AND INNER DIALOGUE

It isn't just Hyper-Creatives who have these internal conversations with their negative top dog. But it may be that the Sergeant Major is more destructive in the lives of Hyper-Creatives than other personality types. In the next chapter we'll look more at the emotional lives of Hyper-Creatives, but for the moment it is enough to know that we have a tendency towards great emotional highs followed by crashing lows. (This might sound rather extreme but you know what I'm talking about!)

At these times of low energy, low motivation and low self-esteem, Sergeant Major Barker can have a field day. Our reserves are reduced and it is harder to counter his attacks. Developing strategies to deal with him during times when you are feeling positive will help you later on when you aren't so self-assured.

You've probably already decided which of the various ideas in this chapter will work best for your personal devil and angel. While you're in a good mood start practising using these techniques because you never know when Churchill's 'Black Dog' of depression could descend…

CHAPTER SIX

WHAT GOES UP MUST COME DOWN

Painters, actors and pop stars are renowned for their huffy fits and excessive expressions of delight. We expect our artists to be depressed, melancholic, manic and, well, a little bit mad. We're not overly surprised to discover that a famous actress has been admitted to The Priory for some much-needed rest or that a poet's most prolific period coincided with heart-break and thoughts of suicide.

We put these mood-swings down to 'the creative temperament'. In our society we have a subconscious recognition that our creative people will be emotionally more expressive. And we understand the connection between this and their work. Is it possible for great art to be created without such an exploration of the dark hidden corners of the psyche? While not all creative types suffer from such emotional extremes, a 1989 study by psychiatry professor Kay Redfield Jamison showed that, compared to the general population, writers and artists have a disproportionate rate of manic-depressive or depressive illness.[18]

You may not be able to draw a bowl of fruit or hit a high C but as a Hyper-Creative you possess many of the same qualities as other creative people. Manic-depression is probably an over-exaggerated name for your condition. But you do not need to be clinically bi-polar to be prone to great highs and lows.

Case study – 'Kat'

When I am down we go through a lot of telephones... because I break them. I'm speaking to someone on the phone and I'm shouting, 'I can't hear you! Bad line!' BANG, BANG, BANG! [Kat indicates that she is smashing the phone on the table at this point]. I'll get on the phone and I am angry about something and in a bad mood and I will feel like a ball of anger and tears. And then my daughter will take me to the cake store and I will be fine. The number one thing the kids are going to say when I am like that is, 'Did you eat?' I am always better when I've had something to eat.

When I get mad, I am mad. And if I can't say something, if someone prevents me from speaking about it, oh gosh!

MADNESS AND CREATIVITY

The link between creativity and madness can be traced back to the ancient Greeks. Dionysus, son of Zeus, was thought to induce madness and frenzied brutality in those around him. The celebrations held in his honour came to symbolize 'creation out of chaos' and were often followed by periods of creative inspiration. In addition, much of the poetry of this time was written for Dionysus.

At the time of Plato and Socrates it was believed that priests and poets communicated with the gods through a kind of madness. And Aristotle asked, 'Why is it that all men who are outstanding in philosophy, poetry or the arts are melancholic?'[19]

During the Renaissance, there was much exploration of the relationship between genius, melancholia and madness, although a distinction was made between the kind of madness that led to creative inspiration and the kind of madness that prevented any kind of achievement being possible. There was a brief moment during the 18th century when it was fashionable to believe that rational thought and balance, rather than emotional extremes and inspiration, were the key elements of genius. However, this was overturned by the time of the Romantics in the 19th century, when anguish, turmoil and brooding were back in fashion and the 'must have' accessory for any budding artiste.

In Jamison's study, 89 per cent of creative writers and artists said they had experienced intense highly productive and creative episodes. One in four reported experiencing extended periods of elated mood before particularly creative periods. They talked about noticing increased levels of enthusiasm, energy, self-confidence, speed of mental association and a strong sense of well-being. At the same time, about 28 per cent noticed pronounced psychological discomfort before a burst of creativity and mentioned anxiety, a general mood of distress and slight paranoia or restlessness.

'Thirty-eight per cent of artists and writers have been treated for mood disorders'

Importantly, when asked about the connection between these moods and their work, nine out of ten said it was integral or, at the very least, important. In contrast with the general population, 38 per cent of artists and writers have been treated for mood disorders (in the wider population the figure is less than 5 per cent). But what do such mood swings (manic depression at its most extreme) and creativity have to do with one another? J. P. Guilford carried out extensive research into creativity and concluded that creative individuals tend to think 'divergently', allowing their thoughts to go in different directions, rather than channelling them. He identified two factors that enabled this kind of creative thinking:

Fluency of thinking: The ability to speak, combine words or develop ideas in a clever, connected or juxtaposed way within a short space of time.

Flexibility of thinking: The ability to produce many ideas that cut across different categories and to come up with unusual solutions to problems.[20]

These same traits are often associated with mania (e.g. lack of focus, the tendency to skip from one subject to another and to be stimulated by a variety of thoughts which seem to come from many different sources). The argument is that when a highly imaginative person's thinking is 'loosened' by a mild manic episode, this will trigger greater creative output from that individual. If increased self-confidence and boldness (also associated with mania) are added into the mix, this can encourage the individual to have greater confidence in their ideas, take more risks, push their ideas forward more vigorously and, sometimes, achieve greater success.

And it isn't just the 'up' part of the cycle that triggers creativity. The 'down' can be a vital ingredient too. Melancholy tends to lead to deeper, more contemplative thinking. Being more critical at these times can assist the creative person in refining or editing their work. Mania tends to produce bursts of intense action; melancholy, a slower, more detailed approach to the work.

And, of course, melancholy can be the trigger for the content of creative work too. Increased sensitivity, emotional pain and questioning of one's place in the universe are the stuff of art and poetry.

The work can also be a treatment or an escape from the moods. Many artists have written of how they were saved from self-destruction by their creative outlet. Lord Byron, who suffered greatly from depression, described the role of poetry in his life:

'It is the lava of the imagination whose eruption prevents an earthquake – they say Poets never or rarely go mad... but are generally so near it – that I cannot help thinking rhyme is so far useful in anticipating and preventing the disorder.'[21]

So how does this all relate to us mere Hyper-Creatives? Well, it is not artistic *talent* that connects mood swings with creative urges. It is not just the likes of Byron, Tennyson and Keats who struggle with their emotional extremes. Thousands of far less talented artists have experienced the same fluctuations in mood and the same fluctuations in creativity. The fact that the work produced by most of these individuals was either overlooked by the Simon Cowells of the past or simply not of a high enough quality to warrant fame and fortune is irrelevant. And just because your creativity manifests itself in ideas rather than poetry, and that these ideas may be more to do with how to meet your team's annual targets while two members of staff are on maternity leave rather than solving the great challenges of the 21st century is also rather immaterial.

For those of us who live with these moods (both high and low) and bursts of creativity, life is something of a roller coaster. We experience events with an intensity that other people may not understand. We can claim to know true joy – the feeling you get when you achieve a goal, when you spend time with a loved one, when you see a great movie – and we have been at the very bottom of the pit too, when we experience extreme disappointment – when life gives us a raw deal or when we are struck by the meaninglessness of some aspect of existence.

Case study – 'Biddy'

My biggest trigger for feeling miserable is not having enough reflection and thinking time. If I feel I am being pushed by someone else's agenda and that I am not in control of my own time I resent it. People often look to me to add structure to their lives, to tell them how to solve a problem and to do that at a time that suits them. If people want to talk to me because they want to talk to me I can be very flexible but when people bring me problems when I am working on something else, I can get very time-precious.

I also get really miserable if it is dark all the time. A day of daylight, for instance, getting out on the bike on a Sunday, works really well for me. I usually bike with friends so people are around me but I am still alone in my helmet so no one can tell me what to think.

And, if we are honest, we wouldn't want to be any other way.

Who wouldn't want to explore the great highs that life can offer? Who wouldn't want to see connections between different subjects and solve problems in new and exciting ways? Who would want to go through life feeling average, having average ideas and average experiences?

In many ways, while we know how tough it is to cope with low energy and low enthusiasm, we would not give it up because we appreciate the flip-side and associated benefits too much.

That's all very well. But might we be limiting our potential by thinking this way?

THE DOWNSIDE OF THE UPS AND DOWNS

The problem with being at the whim of these emotions is that we abdicate responsibility for our own behaviour. At an extreme (and I am sure you don't stoop to this), we use our emotions as an excuse to avoid unpleasant tasks, delay completion, ignore obstacles, even explain away our successes.

So when we wake up in a foul mood – maybe triggered by an actual event but just as likely not – we feel resigned to the fact that we won't be able to overcome it because we get like this sometimes and we can't possibly be expected to do any substantial work today. And this is no ordinary bad mood. Because, as we now know, creative people like us just feel things more intensely. So while someone else may be able to muddle through, we know we get hit harder and therefore we can't just pull ourselves together.

Equally, when we wake up full of the joys of spring, everything seems so rosy that we can't believe it is possible to ever feel badly again. With our pink-tinted glasses on we dismiss all negative voices and ignore warnings. We have no desire to be brought back down to earth. Why would we want that when it feels so good up here?

And because we aren't in control of our emotions we aren't in control of the results. So, if we're in the zone during a meeting and come up with a killer idea, while it feels great, it is hard to take the credit. What if it was a fluke? What if it doesn't happen again?

What if at next week's meeting we're not in the right frame of mind and inspiration doesn't come? The truth is that we are, in fact, much more able to control and affect our emotions than we give ourselves credit for. Perhaps we do feel emotions more intensely than other people as a result of our creativity. But that doesn't mean we cannot take responsibility for our feelings and even change them.

In his bestseller, *The 7 Habits of Highly Effective People*, Stephen Covey outlines his concepts of the 'circle of concern' and the 'circle of influence':[22]

The basic premise is that in our lives there are things we worry about and things we can do something about. So, within our 'circle of influence' are all those issues from the 'circle of concern' that we can affect.

We might not be able to affect the weather (that goes in the circle of concern) but we might be able to anticipate the appropriate clothing to wear so that the weather has less impact on our plans. Instead of spending time damning the rain, we are better utilized purchasing a cagoule. And even when there is nothing practical we can do about an issue that is almost entirely out of our control, what always comes within the circle of influence, according to Covey, is how we choose to deal with those situations. His belief is that we can choose our response.

You will know this yourself: different people will react differently to a similar experience – for instance, being made redundant from their work. One chooses to see this as the end of the world and never really recovers, going from second rate job to second rate job until retirement. The other sees it as an opportunity to make a big change, re-train, start their own business with their pay-off and always reflects that this was the best thing that could have happened.

My father always maintains that having a stroke at the age of 59 was the best thing that could ever have happened. It helped him appreciate life and, what's more, entitled him to a disabled parking badge that he now uses with a flourish at every opportunity. I'm not sure I could be so positive. But then again, when I see the places he is allowed to park there is a tinge of jealousy!

Just because you and I have a natural tendency towards extremes of emotion, it does not give us carte blanche to excuse all our actions as 'out of our control'. Unless you are suffering from a medical condition, you can influence your emotions and use them to your advantage.

This does not mean losing those wonderful highs – you will need them. As we've already discovered, at these times you are likely to be firing on all cylinders and producing some of your best imaginative work. And I'm not talking about losing the lows either – they play their part in making you determined, in helping you explore your inner demons and discover more about yourself which may, in turn, lead to flashes of inspiration. But I am talking about being able to tap into these emotions at the appropriate time and discover all the colours between black and white. Not everything is the 'best in the world' just as not everything is the 'worst in the world'. Some things are just fine. Others are pretty good. And some are not too bad.

Does this sound a bit boring? Prefer to carry on the way you have been, buzzing one moment and crashing the next? Obviously, it is up to you which of the strategies in this book you use to transform your patterns of behaviour and get better outcomes. But working on your 'emotional intelligence' could be a great place to start. It's not that different to upgrading any of the skills you have. After all, if you wanted to pass a maths exam, you might need to learn some advanced equations. And, having practised a bit, you'd find sums that had you baffled a few weeks before suddenly became as easy as 2+2. You can upgrade your emotional intelligence just the same way. All it takes is some guidance and a bit of practice.

CHAPTER SEVEN

BECOME AN EMOTIONAL GENIUS

Your creativity is potentially your biggest asset. Use it well and it will become the key to your success. But in order for that to happen you have to hone it. You have to be able to rely on it when it counts. As long as you are at the whim of your emotions, your creativity will be too. Finding yourself in a grump when you need to be on top form is not an ingredient in the recipe for success.

Improving your 'emotional intelligence' should always be part of anyone's success strategy. According to Daniel Goleman's work on the subject[23], what differentiates exceptional leaders from average ones is largely emotional intelligence, which is measured as an emotional intelligence quotient (EQ). While being very good at their job counts for about a third of their success, two thirds of their success is down to the four elements of emotional intelligence:

Self-awareness: The ability to understand yourself and your reactions, accept feedback and achieve self-confidence.
Self-management: The ability to respond appropriately, be true to your values and adapt to changing circumstances.
Social awareness: The ability to understand other people's feelings, the organization and the customer.
Relationship management: The ability to develop strong relationships with others.

Each of these four main areas can be broken down into 18 more specific emotional intelligence 'competencies'. In this chapter I have only covered eight. The first reason for this is that Goleman and his colleagues have written whole books on the subject, and if you really want to know more you should read one of them. The second reason is that the competencies I have picked out are those that Hyper-Creatives may find most challenging and will benefit most from addressing.

Unlike IQ, EQ levels can be raised (of course we can all make the most of the intelligence we were born with but we can never increase our IQ level). Simply by working on your emotional intelligence you can become more adept. And, as you'll see, improving your EQ will have a direct impact on your success.

EMOTIONAL SELF-AWARENESS

You probably already have a good awareness of your own feelings. You know if you are happy or sad (or devastated or over the moon). This is a good start! In order to develop your emotional self-awareness, however, you also need to know just what triggers these emotions and how they affect your performance. This is probably less obvious. Sometimes you just wake up feeling bad, and sometimes the opposite. However, there is method behind this madness, common denominators behind your change of mood:

- Does tiredness or stress have anything to do with your moods?
- Do certain people or events result in particular feelings?
- Are there some activities that always leave you feeling positive while others always bring you down?

Food, fitness levels, the weather, particular types of work, different kinds of work environment, the time of the day, the time of the month, the time of the year... All of these and more can affect your emotions and having a clearer understanding of the emotional terrain that suits you best will enable you to manage your emotional responses better. If you know that a swim in the morning brightens your day no matter what else is going on in your life, make it your business to swim before an important meeting. If you know that certain people have the uncanny ability to bring you down, either avoid them before you give an important presentation or work with them more closely to develop a communication style that works better for you.

These solutions may sound rather simplistic and, for you, the answers may be more complicated, but that is not an excuse to give up. In fact, the harder it is for you to improve, the greater the pay-off at the end. If this is a big struggle for you, fixing it could transform your performance.

Understanding the implications of your mood on your performance is vital too. While a high, bubbly mood might be appropriate for some kinds of work, you may know yourself to be more effective at other types of work when you are less flamboyant. I find it hard to write when I am very 'up'. I just can't focus. So I either perform other activities at these times (e.g. making phone calls) or I find ways to take the edge off my enthusiasm, such as tidying my desk, sorting out my paperwork, answering my emails and planning my day (as you can see, I am truly a 'structured' Hyper-Creative!). I know from experience that systematic (even boring) work like filing helps me feel balanced again and more level-headed for writing.

Case study – 'Tony'

I've been able to notice now when I am getting the lows and been able to watch them and say, oh, I'm having a bad day. I won't make a decision on that particular day because I am feeling a bit insecure, for whatever reason.

It goes back a few years ago when basically I must have had a breakdown. I'm not sure. I was in debt, there were family problems, business problems. I felt I had bitten off more than I could chew. I had taken a lot of risks. One thing piled on top of another and I couldn't cope with it.

Then we went to California and I sat on the rocks with the seals and I started to feel better. And I decided to learn from the experience and get it right next time. And I've learnt not to have regrets. I just say everything was a learning experience.

SELF-CONFIDENCE

There are times when we are very confident. Some might say egotistical. Whether we admit it to others or not, we know how great we are. Who was it that solved that problem with logistics? Who was it that came up with the new logo? Who was it that found a way through when everyone else thought it was impossible? It was you of course and you are just marvellous.

So how come, 20 minutes after your triumph, you secretly thanked your lucky stars and hoped that you'd be able to come up trumps again? Because creativity can seem like a bolt from the blue, it can also seem random, even accidental. Today you were a hit. Tomorrow you are just as likely to be a miss. Or that's how it feels. And with that unpredictability can come a lack of confidence in yourself.

In addition, we are generally not the only people to judge our ideas. What seemed like a sure-fire winner when you began to explain it to your colleagues, felt more like a dead donkey when you observed the incredulous looks on their faces. It can feel like your ideas are only as good as the last person who judged them. The moment someone says, 'I don't geddit', your confidence can fall apart. And this is important because you need buy-in if your ideas are going to get from your head to the head of department.

A genuinely self-confident person is interested in the opinions of others. They can take critical feedback as well as praise. They are open to changing and adapting their behaviour, their beliefs and their ideas. Truly confident people aren't stubborn. They're people who can afford to say, 'That's an interesting point. I need to think about that some more and maybe make some changes.' They are self-assured enough to learn and grow.

However, they also believe in themselves and value their natural talents. They do not change their opinion of themselves every time a different person expresses a view. They do not bend themselves into uncomfortable pretzel shapes to please others. They fight for what they believe in even when everyone else 'doesn't geddit'. After all, just because others think the idea is rubbish, it doesn't mean they are right.

'Separate criticism of the idea from criticism of you'

Plenty of intelligent people rejected brilliant ideas only to regret their hastiness later. Thomas Watson, the chairman of IBM in the 1940s said, 'I think there is a world market for maybe five computers'. And, of course, The Beatles were rejected by Decca Records in the 1960s because 'The days of groups with guitars are over'.

One way to avoid being torn apart when someone criticizes your idea is to separate criticism of the idea from criticism of you. What are people saying about the idea? And what are people saying about you? The idea may not suit the circumstances – that doesn't mean you were wrong to suggest it. The idea may seem perfect for the circumstances but the market isn't ready for it. That doesn't mean you have lost your touch.

Exceptionally confident people have 'presence'. Think of people you know who are like this. How do they respond to criticism? How do they manage rejection or failure? Ultimately, what you are looking for here is consistency – a level of self-confidence that can be sustained through the ups and downs life throws at you.

Typically, Hyper-Creatives overreact to the opinions of others. It seems to matter very much to us what other people think. (It is, perhaps, because so many of us prefer basing our decisions on our beliefs that we find it so hard for us to receive critical feedback. We just *know* we are right. How dare anyone disagree?) If you have a tendency towards this, learn to keep your mouth shut for an appropriate period of time while you gather your thoughts, access your Higher Self and decide how to proceed. Something like 'Hmmmm, interesting. I need to think about that some more,' said in a neutral, thoughtful tone of voice will buy you some time.

Then you need to simmer down and think about what was said:

- Were the criticisms valid?
- If so, what ideas do you have for adapting to those criticisms?

- If not, what is the evidence to support your original view?
- Is this person's opinion important?
- Do they know what they are talking about?
- Does their lack of experience or naivety give them an insight that more seasoned people lack?

Greater self-confidence (rather than ego) will lead to greater creativity. If you can take onboard the ideas and thoughts of other people, even if they conflict with your own, you will get more material to feed your imagination. A criticism or improvement suggested by someone else could spark you in a whole new direction. And your 'presence' will assist you in persuading others of the merit of your breakthrough concepts.

EMOTIONAL SELF-CONTROL

This is key for Hyper-Creatives. Patience is not a virtue we possess, particularly when we are taken by a new idea. The members of your Success Squad should enjoy these bursts of enthusiasm and be able to handle the crash that follows. But the majority of your colleagues, friends and family will not.

You will probably always find it hard to contain yourself and will need to have an outlet. Extrovert Hyper-Creatives need to talk – otherwise it feels like they will burst. But choose this outlet wisely. You will regret babbling on about your problems to a relative stranger (and maybe already know this from experience). Okay, you may never see them again. And let's hope not. At the first sight of you they will probably turn and run for the hills rather than be subjected to your theories *ad nauseam* again.

Most of the world needs to experience you as calm, positive and composed most of the time. This doesn't mean dropping excitement from your repertoire altogether. It just means responding appropriately. If your tendency is to be black or white, think about all the shades of grey that lie in between. Or, if you find grey a bit dull, think of the colours of the rainbow. You don't have to be red or blue all the time.

Sometimes a simple change of language can help here. Dramatic people tend to use dramatic language:

- 'It was the *worst* day of my life.'
- 'This project is going to be a total *disaster.*'
- 'I'm so psyched. I can barely control myself.' (Often followed by bounding around the room tigger-style.)

There are times when this is absolutely the right response. But every day can't be the worst day of your life and the project probably won't be a total disaster. It just might not be perfect. Adjusting your language to suit the reality of the situation will help you be seen by others as having greater self-control. This is good for your reputation. And it is good for you. Language is a powerful tool. When you say, 'I was so embarrassed I nearly died', your brain believes this is so. The adrenaline starts to rush, your heart beats faster, your voice changes and, before you know it, you are having the physical response of someone whose life was in danger. Saying, 'That was a bit embarrassing' doesn't trigger the same response. And so you remain calm.

ADAPTABILITY

This is particularly relevant for structured Hyper-Creatives. Change is part of life and, increasingly, part of work. Deadlines move, new information is received, clients change their minds, companies grow or shrink or move into new sectors. And sometimes this change happens unpredictably and puts your whole schedule out of whack.

Developing greater emotional self-control will help here (see page 87). In addition, make sure you are alert to the possibility of change. There will be times when there is no warning, but often there are signs. Early on you can adjust your time-scale, build in some excess for later, or just make a mental shift that prepares you for the unpredictable.

Dr Spencer Johnson, in his brilliant little parable *Who Moved My Cheese?*[24] sums the situation up thus:

Accept That Change Happens: Accept that the cheese does move.

Anticipate Change: Prepare for the cheese to move.

Monitor Change: Smell the cheese often so that you know when it's getting old.

Adapt To Change: The quicker you let go of old cheese, the sooner you can enjoy new cheese.

Change: Move with the cheese.

Enjoy Change: Savour the taste of new cheese.

Be Ready To Change Quickly And Enjoy It Again: Accept that the cheese keeps moving.

You can build up a tolerance to change by putting yourself in situations where there is uncertainty. Structured Hyper-Creatives will never *become* flexible Hyper-Creatives by doing this, and will still want to ensure that large parts of their job can be predicted and managed. But exposing yourself to unpredictability on a regular basis will give you the tools to deal with it effectively.

Again, all this is good for creativity. Firstly, to be more successful you need to remain creative during times of change. Building up a tolerance to change will mean you can still operate at full strength during these times.

> **'Build up a tolerance to change by putting yourself in situations where there is uncertainty'**

Secondly, hopefully your ideas will trigger change. One of the reasons you may not have followed through in the past was your discomfort with the realities of the train you had set in motion. The theory was all very well but the practice was another thing entirely.

I dread the major building works that are about to happen in my home. But they are only happening because I had a brainwave about how to transform my surroundings. Basically, I brought disorder upon myself. And I could have stopped at the point where I'd had the idea and never committed to builders and carpenters and plumbers and the rest. But what use would that have been? I'd have had lots of pretty ideas in my head and lots of peeling paint on the walls and threadbare carpets on the floor.

The more I experience change the more accepting of it I become. I will never crave disorder, but I can cope with it just fine.

INITIATIVE

It could be argued that Hyper-Creatives are all about initiative. After all, we're the ones with the talent for problem-solving, often without needing encouragement or a specific instruction to do so. But what happens after that initial spark of inspiration? In terms of emotional intelligence, 'initiative' includes seeking information and taking actions. It's not just about seeing opportunities but acting on them.

Your Success Squad will help you here. They will fill the gaps in the areas where you are weaker or less motivated. But it's up to you to call on their help and take their advice. Sometimes all they can do is encourage you from the sidelines. Only you can make it happen. And here the flexible Hyper-Creatives may struggle. There are steps that need to occur for an idea to come to fruition. Steps are not easy for flexible Hyper-Creatives. But sometimes there is no other way.

Jerry Hirshberg, the founder of Nissan Design International says:

'Business has never been less well-suited to accommodating, let alone stimulating, original thought. Current organizational models revolving around productivity and efficiency at any cost produce a corporate culture hardly conducive to thinking – let alone innovative thinking.'[25]

No wonder you feel like you're swimming against the tide! You may be fortunate enough to work in an organization that embraces lateral thinkers, that understands that creativity doesn't occur 'on demand' and that accepts that it's sometimes better to be late and excellent than on time and acceptable. But, if you aren't and you still want to get to the top, you'll need to learn a bit about structure, just like the structured Hyper-Creative needs to learn to loosen up a bit.

ORGANIZATIONAL AWARENESS

We'd all love to work for a company that had no politics and no historical baggage, where people were self-aware and open to new ideas. But such environments are rare. Even if you set up on your own you will sometimes come into contact with people who have different agendas, make different assumptions and operate using different rule books to you.

You can try to ignore it but you do so at your peril. Understanding the environment in which you work, the culture that has evolved and that guides decision-making, along with the underlying issues that impact behaviour, will enable you to navigate through the obstacles and make your ideas work.

This doesn't mean you have to become a vicious manipulator who uses people to get to the top. It does mean you need to learn about your company and your industry, be well-networked and high-profile, and remain alert to the factors that influence the decision-makers. They will need to be persuaded that your idea will work and you need to know what criteria they are using to judge you. You may be motivated by the desire to improve the lives of your co-workers. They may need to see how the idea will save them money. If you can achieve both, you are on to a winner. If you ignore the fact that they have their bottom line to consider, you will continue to bash your head against a brick wall and wonder why you're getting nothing more than a headache.

INFLUENCE

Very few people can get the attention of the top bods on their own. It will be much easier if there are other people on your side, people who are big fans of yours, who sing your praises, who 'get' you and want to help you. And this is why the ability to 'influence' is so powerful.

Mike Southon and Chris West, in *The Boardroom Entrepreneur*[26], talk about the importance of a 'sponsor' for the 'intrapreneur' (their term for entrepreneurial people who work in larger organizations). They say that no matter how long you've been in the company and how well you know your way around, a sponsor can offer vital advice and open doors that you would struggle to open yourself.

The sponsor may be a formal mentor or just someone you connect with from time to time. And in my view you need not limit yourself to one. One of your 'centres of influence' might be your mentor, but the others can be friends, contacts, colleagues or acquaintances. What is important is that:

- They like you and 'get' you
- They can help you
- They get something back

Step one is to create an 'influence plan' outlining who your centres of influence are (people who can fulfil the three criteria above), how you can meet them or build a stronger relationship with them, and what they would get from such a relationship.

Think of your influence plan as being like a campaign strategy – a way to attract people to you and your 'policies'.

One of the elements of political campaigning that gets under most people's skin is that they never hear from their MP or prospective candidate from one year to the next, and then they're on every street corner and filling your letterbox with paper products as soon as election time comes around.

> **'People who have developed highly effective influence skills use them every day'**

Your campaign strategy should not fall in to this trap. People who have developed highly effective influence skills use them every day. They may not have anything in particular to 'sell'. They're just making contacts, building relationships, helping people out and raising their profile. This means that when they do have an idea that needs a bit of a team effort, the infrastructure is in place.

Hyper-Creatives don't always put in the time necessary to these relationships and when we realize we need them we're like the local councillor who turns up at your door, calls you the wrong name and asks for your vote.

Case study: 'Adrian'

At a party, when I first meet someone, I am terribly entertaining and interested in what the other person is saying. But the next time we meet I do find it very difficult to maintain it. It's to do with my boredom with following through and it happens in my relationships as well as my work. I do have friends I have kept in touch with and I am quite proud of that. But there are also lots of people that I haven't. Far more.

The other problem with an influence plan for Hyper-Creatives is that it is 'a plan'. A plan is hard for many Hyper-Creatives – it involves thinking ahead, designing a series of steps and then taking those steps consistently, over time, without the thrill of immediate pay-offs. In fact, for much of the time it will feel as if you are achieving nothing. You have nothing to show for your efforts. It may even be that you give far more than you receive. At first.

People can spot a selfish networker at 20 paces. If you look like you are schmoozing with one intention – to influence people in high places – then you'll be sniffed out and marginalized. Influence is about developing supporters behind the scenes and you'll only get that if you are genuine. The business networking organization, Business Network International, has a basic premise known as 'Giver's Gain': that is, 'If I give you business, you'll want to give me business.'

The same applies in the corporate world, the public sector or even in your private life. Influence isn't just about getting a high-profile mentor who can pull a few strings while they fill you in on the workings of the upper echelons of your organization. It's about becoming a leading light in your company, taking an interest in what is going on at the top, and at the bottom, becoming a valuable resource who is welcomed into the fold because you have something clever and interesting and helpful to offer. Then, when the time comes and it's you asking for support, you'll find no shortage of allies.

TEAMWORK AND COLLABORATION

We've already looked at creating your own team – your Success Squad – from the kinds of people who love you anyway and for whom you don't need to transform your style in order to be accepted and effective. But what about those people you have to work with whether you like it or not? What about people who have a totally different working style to yours and who can't understand why you're not just like them?

Enhancing your emotional intelligence means developing the ability to get on with other people in a team environment. Like family, you can't always choose your team-mates and there are bound to be differences in style, priorities, even fundamental values.

Highly emotionally intelligent people ask for input from other people – even people who may have conflicting views or approaches. They encourage other people rather than insisting that they are the only ones who can do a particular task. And they build strong relationships based on trust, loyalty and respect.

In fact, 'abrasion', as Jerry Hirshberg terms it in his book, *The Creative Priority*, is a trigger for creativity. When friction occurs, people can be liberated to create something new:

'The prioritization of creativity requires the accommodation of dissent from the prevailing view. While this does not automatically lead to unprecedented thinking, it does open the corporate arteries to the flow of new thoughts. But it requires a tolerance for some real and often threatening discomfort. The abrasion of *creative abrasion* is truly abrasive! It must be, or there would be no challenge to established modes of thought and no opportunity for unprecedented ones.' [27]

So, conflict, discomfort, putting oneself into situations where there will be opposing views, styles and values can create the spark of imagination. Just like rubbing two sticks together to create fire, two people rubbing each other up the 'wrong' way can have the same effect.

But, in order to embrace this, you will have to make a mental shift. You'll need to accept that other peoples' ways of working are just as valid as yours. And you'll have to do this even if they don't grant you the same right. By setting an example, you may influence their behaviour and, eventually, the acceptance you have demonstrated could be returned – but don't hold your breath!

'Like family, you can't always choose your team-mates'

To make this process a little more formalized, and therefore more likely to work out the way that suits you best, you may want to create some team boundaries – standards that you all agree to hold yourselves to.

This doesn't mean disposing of conflict and passionate disagreement, which, as we have already seen, can be a catalyst for new ideas. But it does mean making it safe to do this and agreeing some ground rules so that such abrasion is more likely to result in a breakthrough than a walk-out.

A session where people's gripes and preferences are discussed and where agreement can be made about the basic ground rules that the team abides by can prevent an impasse later on. This is very important for you. To be effective you need a certain environment – one where you can share ideas, work on exciting projects and express enthusiasm. Make sure the boundaries your team creates give you the space to operate at your best, even if you also have to make concessions so that other people with different preferences can do their work too.

Here is the basic process I have developed when helping teams create their ground rules:

1. Provide a clear outline to participants about the purpose of the session in advance. Introverts will need time to gather their thoughts.
2. Make sure the environment is safe, that people are able to express their views without criticism and that there is no such thing as a bad idea.
3. Discuss what kind of team environment you want – if the team were functioning perfectly, what would that look like, feel like, be like?
4. Share what isn't working currently and make sure everyone gets to have their say.
5. Ask what is working currently, ensuring everyone gets all their thoughts across.
6. Now explore 'win-win' strategies – ground rules or boundaries that would assist the whole team in becoming the successful unit everyone described at the start: 'no gossip', 'no teasing', 'honest, open communication', 'ask permission before interrupting' could all be on this list.
7. Keep your final set of ground rules relatively short – 10 statements should be enough – and ensure it is agreed before making it 'official'. You will have wasted your time if some individuals are unconvinced of its value.

Finally, boundaries do need to be enforced. If you are keeping your end of the bargain, you are entitled to remind other people of their commitment. It is best to do this at the time the boundary is breached or as soon after as possible.

There is no need to bring out the big guns at the first sign of a threat. A polite reminder or quiet word will do.

PHEW!

Working on emotional intelligence is really a lifetime commitment – you'll always be looking at ways to upgrade different elements as you face new challenges and different situations. But because EQ is more an art than a science, it isn't going to work out perfectly every time. When you start to change your behaviour you may experience a backlash. People may be confused by sudden changes in you – they may have got used to you being a certain way. They may find some of these changes confusing or suspicious. However, that doesn't mean the benefits also take a lifetime to be felt – a simple change today could have an immediate positive impact.

That's where 'educating your environment' comes in. The best way to avoid suspicion and resistance is to explain to other people what you are doing. This way, if they see a change, they will know the motivation behind it and not assume a hidden agenda. You can even engage their involvement by asking for feedback when they notice you trying something new. Trusted friends and colleagues will be relatively open with you and can help you understand the impact (positive *or* negative) that your behaviour is having on other people and on your own performance and success.

But that's enough of that. Pick an area or two where you feel you would get the most benefit if you improved your EQ and take baby steps if this feels more comfortable. Because there are some other tips that will help you turn your Hyper-Creativity into your biggest asset and they're waiting for you in Chapter Eight.

CHAPTER EIGHT

LEADING THE HORSE TO WATER AND OTHER TRICKS

....

So far I've talked a lot about respecting your natural preferences – knowing what you like and how you operate best and creating an environment that makes the most of it. No matter how hard you work to be more organized (if you are a flexible Hyper-Creative) or to carry out thorough research (if you are a beliefs-driven Hyper-Creative) you will rarely be drawn to this kind of work. To achieve the success that you deserve, you need to respect your innate style and spend as much time as possible working on projects that cash in on your strengths.

Your Success Squad will be a huge help here, supporting you and encouraging you to focus on what you love to do, while they take care of the rest.

In addition, your career decisions may be influenced by this newfound insight into your inner workings. Unless you count 'creative accounting', bookkeeping may not be the best place for a person of your talents because of the need for attention to detail, the repetition, the systems and the vast amounts of data. Some companies may not suit you either. Those that only value practical, by-the-book people who play entirely by the rules will not be the obvious home for you. If you are senior enough you may be able to influence the culture (and companies like that certainly need people like you) but, unless there is a willingness to change the way success is measured, you will be fighting an uphill battle there.

Keep all of this in mind as you read this chapter because it may seem as though I am suggesting you become something other than you are. But I'm not.

What I am saying is that there are times when there isn't anyone else who can implement an idea except you. There isn't anyone else who can write this book, for instance. It has to be me. Somehow I have to make myself sit down every day and do my research, carry out my interviews and put the words on the page.

This means that, even with a great support team, razor-sharp emotional intelligence skills and a reputation for excellence as a creative brain, you will need some tricks to help yourself follow through.

Remember that even the most Hyper-Creative person – i.e. someone with extremely high preferences for extroversion, creativity, beliefs-driven decision-making and flexibility – does, at times, prefer to be introvert, practical, analytical and structured.

While honing the preferences you have most of the time is the priority, honing the preferences you use less frequently comes a close second. At those moments when you know that a timetable is needed or when you have a strong desire to get deeply into a subject through reading and research, you'll want to do these things well.

In addition, you'll want to know what circumstances cause you to act in ways that are not your normal preference. At what times do you feel more introvert? What kinds of activity bring out your attention to detail? When do you get excited about making a plan?

And my final word of preparation for this chapter is this: we don't always get to do exactly what we want to do all the time. No matter how carefully you have designed your life and how seriously you take the concept of natural preferences, there are times when you will have to undertake activities that are necessary and important to your success but aren't a comfortable fit.

THE PROBLEM WITH 'FOLLOW THROUGH'

It isn't just Hyper-Creatives who struggle to finish what they start. It is the human condition. Even though we know what's 'right' we often end up doing what's 'wrong'.

So we all know that exercise and healthy eating will keep us alive and fit for longer. Yet most people who start exercise programmes quit. You'll know from television programmes like *DIY SOS* that thousands of people every year start demolishing walls in their house and erecting shelves, only to find the job overwhelming. People start evening classes, take up new hobbies, plan exciting trips abroad and lose steam before achieving their goal.

Steve Levinson and Pete Greider, in *Following Through*[28], say that the problem lies with the fact that we have two 'guidance systems' for making decisions that work in completely opposite ways.

The 'primitive guidance system' responds to events in the moment: there's an impulse followed by a response. Humans are, in part, guided by this system and so are animals. In the animal world even a seemingly thoughtful action like a squirrel saving acorns for winter is not a decision, it's instinct. Mr Nutkin isn't thinking, 'It's a bit cold today. I should probably start thinking about gathering acorns.' He just does it when he is exposed to the right conditions.

By this argument, if you were exposed to the right conditions and were operating according to your primitive guidance system you would always be motivated to do the right thing based on instinct. You wouldn't continue to eat when you were already full. Your primitive guidance system would kick in and you would stop. You wouldn't watch television all day Saturday when you knew you needed some exercise. You would be out there jogging through the streets because your body told you it was right. You'd have in-built knowledge just like the squirrel does about how to keep yourself alive and the motivation to do it. No decision-making would be needed. An impulse leads to action.

Humans do have this system. It's the instinctive part of us that knows what's best for us. It is the part that responds to what is happening in the present moment. Got an itch? Scratch it. Hungry?

Get some food. Need to get fit? Do some exercise. But if we know what's good for us through our instincts, why don't we always do what's good for us?

Unlike animals, humans also have an 'intelligence-based guidance system'. This is the bit that allows us to analyze, think and figure out what to do. It is vital to our survival, as it allows us to adapt to changing circumstances. When roads were first built we learnt the importance of looking both ways before crossing. Hedgehogs will never learn this lesson no matter how many of them meet an untimely death as a result. The problem is that while the 'intelligence-based guidance system' helps us to think it doesn't help us to 'do'. We may have great intentions but we also have the choice about whether to ignore those intentions.

'We may have great intentions but we also have the choice about whether to ignore those intentions'

To make things worse, the two guidance systems are continually working at cross-purposes. The intelligence-based system helps us figure out the best course of action in the long run. The primitive system reacts to present day conditions. They do not co-operate. They act independently. But the primitive system is very powerful: the needs or desires of the moment are more compelling than our well thought-out ideas about what we 'should' do for our long-term benefit.

What this means in practice is that we don't always do what we should because instant gratification is more compelling. Our intention is to read mind-enhancing novels in the evenings instead of watching television. But *CSI: Crime Scene Investigation* is on at 9pm and the book can wait until tomorrow, so guess which one we choose?

For Hyper-Creatives the problem is more extreme because we have so many good ideas, so many good intentions. Our motivation levels are so high at the start and our plans so grand that it is even more noticeable when we get halfway and give up.

Ideas on their own are worth little. Their only value, apart from the fun of coming up with them, is seeing the best ones turned in to real substance. So if our big gift is ideas and yet, because of these competing guidance systems and our natural tendency to avoid the nitty-gritty, mundane, repetitive, hard graft, none of them make it to fruition, how exactly have we added value to the world?

That's why we need to understand how to make these guidance systems work in our favour. In a sense we have to trick ourselves into doing the right thing, so that we can make the most of what we have to offer.

EMERGENCY CRASH PROCEDURE

Whenever one embarks on a journey that is considered a little risky (getting on a plane, boarding a cruise ship, hiking up Kilimanjaro) we're obliged to listen, in silence, to the safety announcement. The Emergency Crash Procedure is explained to you as the plane begins to move along the runway (by which point it is already too late to change your mind and keep your feet on *terra firma*). And that is the point to an extent. You're already travelling down a particular path. It's a bit risky. You know that. But you want to go on that two-week all-inclusive to Florida so much that you'll live with the tiny risk of crash-landing in the ocean.

When you embark on a project, you know there is a risk that you will not complete it. Your Hyper-Creativity, combined with your conflicting guidance systems, means that you don't always reach your destination. In that instance you'll need your own Emergency Crash Procedure – a known, systematic set of steps that protects you and, if used effectively, ensures the plane keeps spluttering (maybe even gliding) just long enough to get you to the terminal.

The crew know when it is time to put the Emergency Crash Procedure into action. There are certain criteria that, when met, mean every step after that is automatic. The masks drop down, the emergency lights come on, everyone in the toilets is told to return to their seat.

In the same way you not only need your own set of procedures, but you also need to know when they should be put into operation. The following questions will help you identify your pattern, your triggers and your equivalent to the flashing seat-belt sign. When these factors come into play it is time to assume the emergency crash position.

When do you start to lose focus?

This won't just depend on how Hyper-Creative you are. It is not the case that people with a very high extrovert, creative, beliefs-driven and flexible preference will give up any earlier than someone who is borderline Hyper-Creative. It depends on what skills you have developed already, the type of work you are doing and your mood. However, you may recognize a pattern. Do you start losing momentum right before the final hurdle, shortly after you begin or somewhere in the middle? Be as specific as possible.

What is the signal that you are losing steam?

Do you start prioritizing other activities or going for 'quick wins' rather than continuing to work on your longer-term project? You may notice that, at the start, you kept to a disciplined timetable and ignored any other calls on your time but after three weeks you started to compromise, allowing meetings, phone calls, emails, longer lunch breaks or 'more urgent priorities' to send you off track.

Your signal might also be that you start going off your original idea. Perhaps you notice that your energy levels drop, you start finding fault, you hope no one will ask you about it because you've become bored of the concept.

Alternatively, you may continue to work on the project but start cutting corners, losing attention to detail, skimping on the research. You may even believe you have just become more efficient, but the truth is you just aren't doing such a good job.

What is your pattern of highs and lows?

As we discussed in Chapter 6 (see page 74), Hyper-Creatives live life on a roller-coaster. Sometimes we're up, sometimes we're down, and there is normally a pattern related to the time of year, the time of month, the day of the week or the time of day. Sometimes the pattern is triggered by the weather, by certain comments from other people that always bring you down or by various events coinciding, which individually you could handle but together add up to a trigger.

Often a great high is followed by a great low. While you might not want to admit it, the time to prepare for a crash is while you are high. This doesn't mean bringing yourself down (you may not want to or even be able to) but it

'The time to prepare for a crash is while you are high'

might mean putting in place some strategies to catch you when, sooner or later, you do inevitably feel the dark clouds approach.

Specifically what types of job cause you to splutter to a halt?

Two types of work might seem very similar but trigger a very different response in you. Walking to the shops and walking on the treadmill at the gym both involve... yes, walking. But one may hold much more appeal for you than another. What's the difference? And what does this tell you about your natural preferences? It isn't the walking that's important. It's the fact that in one case there is an immediate pay-off (you reach the shops and buy that Danish you've been fantasizing about) and in the other you walk and walk and get nowhere. Alternatively, in one case you walk while thinking, 'Why am I bothering? I could have just jumped in the car,' and in the other you're thinking, 'Great – 40 minutes without the children, the telephone or email. Bliss.'

Concluding that it's paperwork that causes you to grind to a halt is like saying you don't enjoy walking. There may be some types of paperwork, at certain times or in a certain environment that you fly through. So, what really triggers energy drain? Once you know you can predict your behaviour and take evasive action.

Case study: 'Mike'

Very often I get scared about money and about old age. I get myself into a panic about the financial consequences of my choices. I know that at this point I get drawn back into the corporate existence even when I have begun to take quite bold strides towards something else.

For instance, acting. I found a way to turn my interest in acting into a business so that I could pay the mortgage and have a decent car to drive around in. It is a war of attrition where the big idea to become an actor gets worn away by the security of mediocrity. So I will pull back to the mediocre rather than take the big risk and go for what I really want.

Answering questions like those above is like learning to read the altitude gauge. You begin to recognize patterns of behaviour that indicate that you are about to go off track or lose power. Now you'll need some strategies for a safe landing, so let's explore some of your options.

BURN YOUR BRIDGES

Earlier in this chapter I referred to the times when you had behaved in ways that were not your normal preference. These are the times when you did finish what you started, when you were thorough, when you felt calm and balanced and ticked all the boxes.

Often we do this when there is basically no other choice – for instance, staying up all night to write an essay because it is due in at 9am the next day. You have left yourself no other option but to get on with it and your two guidance systems are finally working in tandem. The intelligence-based system has been saying for some time, 'You'd better write that essay,' and the primitive system is saying, 'You have to do it right now.'

Levinson and Grieder tell the story of a man and his son who are camping in the woods. A werewolf appears from nowhere and bites the father's leg, then disappears again. The father knows that, come nightfall, he will become a werewolf too and possibly hurt his son. So while it is still light, they build a cage together. The father's instructions to the son are clear: 'Whatever happens, do not let me out of this cage until day-break.'[29]

He makes it impossible to do the wrong thing. He taps into the immediacy of the moment to prevent himself acting wrongly later on. He burns his bridges so the only way he can behave is the right way (in this case, he can't hurt his own son).

Locking yourself in a cage probably isn't the answer for the challenges you face. But you might be able to apply the principle of burning your bridges to a task that needs your on-going commitment.

The key is to find out what will stop you going back on your word. What is it that stops you acting 'wrongly' and keeps you on the straight and narrow?

Case study – 'Sophie'

I don't mind hard slog if there is a sense of achievement for me at the end. A lot of my decisions about where to put my energy have to do with my level of interest. If a particular activity has direct benefit for me and my team, it gets done.

Other than that, I probably assess who are the people that are important and prioritize what I need to do to satisfy them. My criteria for deciding what to finish to a really high quality is based on an assessment of whose opinion matters to me most.

There are some people you don't always have to do stuff for.

AVOIDANCE TACTICS

You may consider yourself the master of avoidance. You've got it down pat. Somehow you've managed to get away with not finishing the tiling in the bathroom, not achieving your targets at the gym and not submitting that report to the boss. But in this context you're going to use your acute avoidance skills for 'good'.

For me, one of the worst things a person can say is that I have disappointed them. I really hate to let people down and do something that lowers their opinion of me. Call it pride or ego or the need to please, I will avoid disappointing others at all costs, even if it means behaving in ways that are not my natural preference.

I use this to my advantage when I have a job or a project, which I really need to complete. I tell people about it. For me this serves two functions. As an extrovert it means I get my need to talk about what I am doing met. And it means I

'Avoidance is a powerful motivator, because it has an immediate pay-off'

have witnesses that I am answerable to. In truth, these people could probably not care less whether I did what I said I would do. They are probably quite used to people saying they will do something and then not following through. And they probably won't think less of me if I behave the same way. But it isn't about them. It's about me and my internal workings. I want to be able to say, 'Yes, I did it,' rather than, 'Actually, I never got around to that.'

You may be like this too. More likely you have your own 'avoid at all costs' outcomes. This is where a 'need to be liked', a 'need to be the best', a 'need to be admired' or a 'need to surprise' (I could go on) come in very useful.

Most people are more 'away from'-motivated than 'towards'-motivated: i.e. we will do X in order to avoid Y but we might not do X in order to achieve Z. Avoidance is a more powerful motivator. This is partly because avoidance has an immediate pay-off and therefore plays into our primitive guidance system. If I want to avoid disappointing other people I get an immediate boost every time someone asks how I am getting on with my project and I can say, 'Really well, thanks.'

Although I realize that I will have a great sense of achievement once my project is done, that pay-off may be a month, a year or a decade away. I can't wait that long! Such a long-term achievement doesn't mean anything to me. No matter how much I visualize, daydream or create a collage depicting the end-point, my primitive guidance system really only cares about the here and now. And my intelligence-based system is giving me all the reasons not to follow through.

Relying on my keen desire to avoid disappointing people is a more effective technique than believing that this time I will be able to stay focused on the long-term benefit, even though that has never worked for me before.

Thinking back on times when you have followed through you may notice a common thread – something that motivates you, which is not simply 'getting the job done'. Perhaps the reason for completion was nothing to do with the project itself. Maybe you were trying to impress a member of the opposite sex. Maybe the process was so fun that the objective became irrelevant. Maybe you were trying to avoid disappointing others, personal discomfort or something you wanted to do even less than the project at hand. All of these success strategies have something in common. You do the right thing but not necessarily for the right reason. And, quite frankly, who cares? As long as you get something important done, the reasons you did it are rather irrelevant.

Case Study – 'Biddy'

Treats! That's how I get myself to do things I don't want to do. It happened yesterday. I was working at home and I had to pack up some clothes. It is a very hard thing for me to do, so I promised myself cheese on toast for lunch as a reward.

It didn't work perfectly because I cheated and gave myself cheese on toast just before I finished. Eventually I did get it done, after lunch and a chat with Katie, who helps around the house.

The other thing that helps is knowing someone else is doing a worse job than me. Katie was cleaning the kitchen, which is far worse. I couldn't let her down by not doing my part and finishing the packing.

LEADING THE HORSE TO WATER

You can lead a horse to water but you can't make it drink. That's true. But also, a horse can't drink, even if it wants to, if it isn't near water. Levinson and Greider explain that motivation is much easier when you put yourself in a better position to do a task.[30] You can't make the horse drink but you can make it easier for him to drink. You can help with the first step.

The same applies to you. There will be tasks you don't want to do. But you can make them as easy to do as possible. Here are some of the ways to make a tough job easier:

Break it down: This old classic is still a winner. You may not be able to do a whole day of invoicing. But you may be able to do one invoice a day for a week.

Make it comfortable: Instead of doing your least favourite jobs at your desk, do your least favourite jobs in front of the television, with friends, sitting in the garden or with a cup of tea and a slice of cake.

Reward yourself: Line up a series of little rewards to mark even the smallest step forward.

Don't look ahead – just do the next step: Thinking about the whole project may be overwhelming but thinking only about the next step is manageable. So just move from A–B rather than A–B–C–D–argh!

Two steps forward and one step back is still one step forward: Being too hard on yourself following a little slip is self-defeating. Long-term it is not effective to motivate yourself (or anyone else for that matter) using only the stick approach. Beating yourself up for slipping back into old habits will not help you overturn those old habits. Instead, allow yourself to take a step back but then concentrate on taking a step or two forward.

THE '5 MINUTES FAST' METHOD

Some people set their watch five minutes fast so that they are always five minutes early.

The problem is that you can only trick yourself with this one for so long before you start saying, 'I don't need to leave yet. My watch is five minutes fast.'

But the principle is a useful one: for example, if you have a large project to do, which would involve doing two actions a day to complete by the deadline, set your goal at three actions a day. This way you will at least meet the deadline, if not complete the project early.

> **'At the start of a project, compile a set of criteria that need to be met if the project is going to be a success'**

Because we get wise to our own tricks you'll need to ring the changes from time to time but you can use your creativity to come up with different ruses. That's the fun bit!

USE WHAT YOU'VE GOT

As I've pointed out before, whatever your preferences are you'll still be attracted to the opposite at times. In addition, your profile might contain a useful preference, which helps you mitigate against some of the challenges of being Hyper-Creative.

Analytical Hyper-Creatives

Use your preference for facts and data to balance out your flexibility. Your flexibility encourages you to ignore deadlines and stray from your path. But your analytical head can help you compile a convincing case for staying on track. The facts tell you that 1 August is absolutely the last day for working on this project. By all means use your flexibility but trust the facts and do not go beyond that date.

You can also use your analytical mind to identify success criteria. At the start of a project, compile a set of criteria that need to be met if the project is going to be a success. Ask yourself, 'For this project to be complete, what needs to happen? What targets do we need to achieve? What standards must we meet?'

There will be research involved in this. It will also make use of your ability to make decisions in a detached, unemotional way. A beliefs-driven Hyper-Creative will find this difficult, as 'success' will be reliant on how they and others 'feel'. For you, success can be measured by a set of objective criteria. This will also help manage your flexible tendencies, as you will have decided in advance what completion looks like and you will therefore know when you get there. Consequently you are less likely to go beyond the deadline.

Structured Hyper-Creatives
Use plans, schedules and tick-boxes to get you to your destination. Set aside time for planning and managing the rest of your time, so that you keep on top of the detailed work.

Create, or get someone else to create, processes that keep you on track. Because you enjoy getting organized, having a process, a pro-forma or a colour-coded system will make you feel on top of what you are doing. You may not be able to develop these yourself, but once you have them you will use them quite consistently.

All Hyper-Creatives have the tendency to get bored, however, so when you notice you are using these structures less effectively it is time to upgrade them or re-invent them. They will probably need it anyway.

Beliefs-driven/flexible Hyper-Creatives
Identify the times (or types of work) where you are naturally structured or analytical. Build these into any project. For instance, if you are most analytical early on, while you are still excited and positive, do your research then. Later on you will find it much harder to focus on the detail. If you are more likely to be structured first thing in the day, set aside half an hour every morning to plan your work. Create (or have someone else create) a pro-forma, which you always use, so that later on, when your motivation levels fall, it is as easy as possible to do your planning – you just have to fill in the boxes.

USE YOUR CREATIVITY

Whatever else happens, you are fortunate enough to be creative. This means you can take these tricks and make them your own or, of course, develop completely original strategies. There are times when your Success Squad can't complete a project for you – you'll have to overcome your natural tendency to avoid certain types of work. But exactly how you interpret and refine the ideas in this chapter is up to you. Just remember:

- At times you will have a preference for 'flip-side' activities, such as detailed, repetitive tasks.
- At times everyone finds it hard to finish what they start – not just Hyper-Creatives.
- At times you will have to work in ways that are not your preference. Keep these to a minimum but recognize when it is unavoidable.

It is a cliché, but only because it is true – doing what you've always done is not good enough. It will get you the same results it always has. Those results are fine if what you want to do is stay exactly where you are. But I am assuming you want to develop and become more successful. That will mean developing a set of strategies that work for you when there is no other option and you have to operate outside your preferences.

We've spent enough time looking at how to effectively do what you don't really enjoy doing. How about we spend some time looking at what you really love and how you can share your gift with the world?

CHAPTER NINE

GIVING THE GIFT OF CREATIVITY – PART 1: THE CREATIVE ORGANIZATION

As you know, not everyone finds it as easy as you to be creative. Just think of how many meetings you have sat through watching other people become obsessed with cleaning under their fingernails, a little spot on the ceiling or shuffling their agenda the moment the group is asked for ideas.

Those four little words – 'Let's have a brainstorm' – fill many people with dread. They know that they will be called on to be original at the drop of a hat. Their ideas will need to be realistic or else they will be rejected out of hand. And then, if someone's idea does hit the mark, there is worse to come. Because ideas mean change and change is bad. And it's not just individuals who baulk at the idea of ideas – businesses do too...

Jerry Hirshberg, the founder of Nissan Design International and author of *The Creative Priority*, says that while business should be all about ideas, business structures actually stifle them[31]. Without ideas a business cannot be created: business, as he puts it, starts with an idea. And yet, 'a traditional bureaucratic structure with its need for predictability, linear logic, conformity to accepted norms and the dictates of the most recent long-range "vision statement" is a nearly perfect idea-killing machine.'

It is likely that even you dread the announcement of a brainstorm meeting under conditions like these. Yes, creative geniuses like us enjoy sparking off other people and developing ideas. If we could spend the whole day with like-minded people, exploring crazy, ground-breaking, top of the head, even downright ridiculous, concepts, we'd be in heaven. But brainstorming is rarely like that.

In most organizations today, even when ideas are asked for, creativity is conditional:

- There is a time and a place for ideas. This is generally at a meeting and often during a specific point in the meeting, for instance 'Any Other Business'.
- Ideas must be realistic. An idea that ignores financial constraints, limited human resources and industry cultural norms is not appropriate.
- Ideas must be fully formed. They are open to immediate scrutiny and, if they cannot withstand such criticism, they are deemed to be worthless.
- The idea must be robust enough to make it through the bureaucratic hoops into fruition. This may mean getting buy-in from powerful people who are threatened by change, who are threatened by you or who simply don't get it.

And that's just for starters.

Hirshberg's challenge at NDI (now Nissan Design America – NDA) was to design an organization around creativity, rather than simply making room for creativity. He understood from his years in the automotive industry that creativity isn't something that happens in isolation and on demand, and therefore a truly creative organization must have a basic structure that enables ideas to bubble up at any moment.

The need for ideas in his business was clear. Design sells cars and design is seen as inherently creative. That's not to say he didn't have a challenge on his hands. Even though he was asked to create this centre of excellence in the field of design where one would think ideas were valued, he had to overcome many common assumptions that inhibited creativity.

For instance, at General Motors, his previous employer, each GM brand of car was designed in a different studio. Cadillac was sealed off from Chevrolet and the guys from Pontiac did not co-operate with the team from Buick. The argument was that each studio would be more creative because competition had been set up between them. Working in isolation from one another they would not be influenced by what other studios were doing and therefore would be able to originate totally new concepts.

> '**Hirshberg realised that secrecy led to very little differentiation... so he encouraged the stealing of ideas**'

The reality was that an environment of protectionism was created. People had to hide their ideas from others. Career advancement rested on individual achievement and therefore there was nothing to be gained by collaboration. When Hirshberg was re-thinking this structure he realized that competition and secrecy between studios actually led to very little differentiation between products because it did not harness the true potential of creative talent. At NDI he encouraged the stealing of ideas. If a designer was inspired by a colleague's idea he could work on it himself and take it in a new direction. The only restriction was that he must credit the originator of the idea and must be willing to have his own ideas stolen in return.

Procter & Gamble has also rethought the way it develops new product ideas. It realized that relying on its internal R&D department to drive innovation was no longer sufficient. It needed to grow by $4 billion a year just to survive. The 'invent-it ourselves' model was no longer viable.[32] So it decided to look outside, estimating that for every P&G researcher there were 200 scientists or engineers in the world who were just as good.

The company would tap into the talents of outsiders and change the culture of the company from one that resisted 'not invented here' ideas, to one that embraced those that were 'proudly found elsewhere'.

But companies such as Nissan, P&G and the others I mention in this chapter, are exceptional. Most organizations have not re-thought the way they design and develop new products. And, of course, creativity need not be marginalized to those in creative roles or industries.

In any company a proportion of people have the job of looking ahead, developing new products and services, designing packaging and imagining the future of the organization and the industry as a whole. But most people who work in the company are not involved in these activities directly. They answer the phones, provide customer service, carry out the administration, manage a team, make sales, maintain the IT equipment, do the day-to-day delivery of the service provided... Just because you are a creative thinker, doesn't mean you are an inventor of gadgets or a talented product designer.

Case study – 'Biddy'

I never thought of myself as creative because I don't do art or writing. But I work in an organization that makes a difference to people's lives. As a librarian in a university I have terrific opportunities to make a difference, have an impact.

My creativity is focused on enhancement, bringing education to people who might not think of going to university, using my skills to do things other people might not think of. My skill is to do things other people couldn't do or thought were impossible.

There is a place for creative thinking in every corner of the business. Mike Southon and Chris West believe that wherever there is 'pain' there is an opportunity for creative thinking.[33] So where is the pain in your area of work?

- Does red-tape and paperwork restrict efficiency?
- Is there a high staff turnover because there is little opportunity for professional advancement?
- Is the office too noisy?
- Is there inconsistency in the way individuals are rewarded or recognized?
- Do visitors to the site seem slightly lost and uncomfortable?
- Are days filled with meetings where decisive action is rarely agreed?
- Do customers stay with you long-term, or do they go elsewhere after a short period of time?
- Has a new competitor just entered the market?

And just as creativity should not be limited to small portions of the business, creativity should not be limited to a small portion of the people.

In their *Harvard Business Review* article 'Managing for Creativity'[34], Richard Florida and Jim Goodnight write about the principles developed at software company SAS to encourage peak performance from creative people. They claim that professionals whose primary responsibilities include innovating, designing and problem-solving – the creative class – make up a third of the US workforce and take home nearly half of all wages and salaries. And so, looking after their best interests must also be in the interest of the business.

Whether you are officially in this class because you have a creative role or because you apply your natural preference for creativity in a broader way doesn't matter. What matters is that you already have a gift that makes a difference in the business world, if you use it effectively. You can make yourself even more valuable if you use that gift to bring out the creativity in the people around you, and if you use it to transform the very culture of your company from one that marginalizes ideas to one that makes ideas a foundation stone – not just making room for ideas but designing the organization *around* them.

SURELY THAT DILUTES MY USP?

One would think so! Just as one would think that keeping Pontiac designers away from Cadillac designers would lead to more originality and differentiation and that sourcing ideas from within P&G must be better for business than buying in ideas from outside.

The benefits to you of sharing your gift are multiple:

- You get to lead this. You raise your profile by turning your natural desire/need for a more creative environment into a practical benefit the company can see. You are no longer the weirdo in the corner who comes up with all the crazy ideas. You are now someone who is committed to enhancing creative skills within the organization. This is much better for your reputation.
- You will be able to perform better if the environment in which you work is attuned to creativity. At present you are fighting a culture that suffocates ideas. By building creativity into the culture your ideas will be valued more highly. It will also be much more fun for you.
- You'll have people to spark off. It is much easier to create when other people are creating too.
- This can only improve your creative ability. Your natural preference for ideas won't be diminished if other people learn to use theirs more effectively. You may have to raise your game to distinguish yourself but you've got all the innate talent. Instead of swimming against the tide, you will be in an environment that is willing to invest in honing your skills because it realizes the value of people like you.

WHAT COMES FIRST – THE CHICKEN OR THE EGG?

You can take one of two approaches here. You can either look at the fundamentals of the organization and how these could be transformed to create an environment that welcomes and nurtures ideas. Or you can focus on the people closest to you, taking more of a micro, incremental approach by coaching, supporting, mentoring and suggesting.

Your choice will be based on how much influence you have. You might like to radically transform the business from its core but that's hard to do when you are a part-time PA. You may also want to use your immediate network (your colleagues, team or department) to pilot your plan, ironing out kinks and gaining evidence of the impact of this newly-formed creative corner of the company before trying something more radical.

Having said that, you may want to go right to the top with this. In order to be sustainable, a change like this ultimately needs support from on high.

I'll let you decide! In this chapter we'll look at some of the fundamental elements of the creative organization. In the next we'll look at how to coach and coax the creativity out of the individuals around you.

WHAT DO CREATIVE ORGANIZATIONS LOOK LIKE?

Every organization that has a genuinely creative culture has achieved it in a different way. Pulling together every variation would be a book in itself. So, I have drawn out themes that you may be able to interpret for your own organization. They can either be implemented wholesale, or, of course, used as an inspiration for you to develop fresh, original ideas that suit the realities of your situation perfectly.

They create sparks

When we are asked to imagine the perfect team, we generally describe a utopia where all members get along, enjoy each other's company, invite one another over for dinner and would gladly spend time together anyway. But such an environment is rare (okay – I've never found it – have you?) and actually not conducive to creativity. Very often you will have a new idea when you bring two or more unrelated thoughts together in a light-bulb moment. This can also happen between people when their conflicting points of view collide – the 'creative abrasion' we covered earlier. When creative abrasion is used effectively, neither person's point of view dominates. Instead, the friction is noticed and signals an opportunity for creative problem-solving.

Creative organizations aren't afraid of this kind of conflict. In fact, they encourage it. At Nissan, Hirshberg organized designers into divergent pairs: for instance, he would team up a 'detail person' with a 'big picture person' (very like the

'Sparks will fly. But so will fresh thinking and new approaches to age-old problems'

Success Squad model, although here not only to balance their differing preferences but also to generate sparks).

Such friction is particularly powerful when people have a similar specialization but divergent points of view. They trust each other because they recognize the legitimacy of the other people around them, which enables them to lower their resistance to both criticism and alternative approaches to solving a problem.

However, bringing together specialists from different parts of the business to work on a challenge can be powerful too. What if the marketing team were involved (as equal partners) in product development alongside the designers? What if the IT department worked hand in hand with the Finance Director's team to co-create the future growth of the business? Yes, they have different priorities. Yes, they have a different agenda. Yes, sparks will fly. But so will fresh thinking and new approaches to age-old problems.

Of course, sometimes conflict can become dysfunctional. In fact, most examples of conflict you have seen could probably be considered unhealthy. In order to develop a culture that recognizes conflict as an opportunity for creativity there needs to be some ground rules.

It helps if there is a shared vision for what must be achieved. When targets and outcomes are agreed, any conflict happens within this context. Members of a team working on a project trust that everyone is trying to get to the same place. The conflict is only over *how*.

'When a company becomes too congenial, it becomes complacent'

Of course, agreeing the shared vision may be where conflict first arises. In this case, the team or organization has to take a step back and settle for some other aspect on which to agree. Agreeing the values of the organization or developing some ground rules about how the inevitable conflict will be handled may be a place to start.

I think of this preparation stage as being like a safety net above which the trapeze artists can practise, take risks, even fall. There may be disagreements about how to catch your partner, what will work and what will not, but at least no one will break their neck.

This kind of conflict also prevents what I call the 'Galapagos Islands Syndrome'…

The Galapagos Islands are famous for the unique and varied life forms found there. Untouched by human beings for almost all of their history, the islands' inhabitants evolved in ways that were ideally suited to their environment, unsullied by migrating creatures from other environments. However, when humans did arrive, the living things they discovered were not well adapted to coping with the sudden threat. Many became extinct within a short period of time until conservationists stepped in and called a halt to the destruction of this special environment.

The same thing can happen in organizations. When a company becomes too congenial, it becomes complacent. The employees of the company develop their own culture, values and ways of thinking. They believe that they continue to reflect the range of views found in the outside world but as time goes on they become more and more isolated from the real world and a sub-culture evolves. It ignores (or is ignorant of) threats on its doorstep and is totally unprepared when it finally realizes that the world has changed while its back was turned.

Without abrasion, challenge and a level of conflict, companies become like the Galapagos Islands, happily getting on with life in the mistaken belief that everything is fine. Creative organizations are never complacent. They are always asking questions, challenging assumptions and taking risks. Through this process they anticipate what is around the corner and lead the way rather than waiting to be invaded by turtle-eating pirates.

This is not to say that genuine conflict should be encouraged and the root causes of personality clashes should not be dealt with. As mentioned earlier, competition and petty rivalry does not lead to innovation, it leads to protectionism and secrecy. Just because you have lots of fights at work doesn't mean you have a highly creative environment.

But in a situation where conflicting opinions naturally arise or are created intentionally in a safe and suitable environment, there is an opportunity. After all, it is the sparks in an engine that cause it to run and the grinding of grains of sand in an oyster shell that creates the pearl.

They allow or encourage failure

Did you ever wonder why there's always a guy who seems to get the girls even though he's rather plain, rather dull and rather average in every way? If you ask him, and he decides to be honest, he'll probably tell you that he just asks a lot of girls. Even with a low rate of success, he's guaranteed to get lucky a small percentage of the time. The more girls he asks, the luckier he seems to get.

Perhaps a more appropriate example of the value of failure is the quote by Thomas Watson, the founder of IBM: 'The fastest way to succeed is to double your failure rate.'[35]

As you will know, not all of your ideas are good. In fact, some are downright awful. But, if you've been experimenting with creativity all your life, you will know that you can't censor yourself or you will also lose the brilliant gems.

In an environment where mistakes are allowed – even encouraged – people take risks. And, in taking risks, they make discoveries. Thomas Edison didn't get the light bulb right first time; in fact, he didn't get it right until the very last time. (Edison did not actually invent the light bulb *itself*, though he was instrumental in producing a new concept: a high resistance lamp in a very high vacuum that would burn for hundreds of hours. While the earlier inventors had produced electric lighting in laboratory conditions, Edison concentrated on a commercial application and was able to sell the concept to homes and businesses by mass-producing relatively long-lasting light bulbs and creating a system for the generation and distribution of electricity. The reason I explain all this is (1) I don't want lots of letters telling me I got my facts wrong and (2) this story demonstrates how creativity can be used to refine and upgrade something that already exists. It doesn't just apply to creating something brand new.)

In failure-tolerant organizations, success and failure are treated the same way. There might be just as much to learn from a success as there is from a failure. Sometimes something works but it is a fluke. Sometimes something works and we really need to know why so that we can replicate it. Sometimes something works but it can be better. Organizations that are risk- and failure-averse also ignore successes.

When I worked as a producer at the BBC, we would have daily post-mortems to discuss the programme we had just broadcast. A common comment was: 'That didn't work very well. What went wrong?' followed by a pointed look in the direction of whoever was responsible for the item. However, a question I don't ever recall hearing was: 'That worked well. What was so good about it?' Ralph Keyes and Richard Farson say that perfunctory praise (i.e. simply saying, 'Well done!') actually demotivates people[36]. Combining such praise with questions, feedback and a genuine expression of interest, however, is much more motivational. And, by analyzing success in the same way as we analyze failure, the distinction between the two becomes eroded.

Failure can be expensive and I am certainly not encouraging you to intentionally make mistakes any more than I am encouraging you to intentionally develop enemies in order to provide opportunities for creative abrasion. However, by treating failure differently (and in turn treating success differently), you can start to have an impact on the culture in your team or organization.

They make time for play

We all know that our best ideas don't come while we're staring at our computer screens. So how come so many organizations insist on staff being present at their desk for upwards of eight hours a day?

'As time pressure increases, creative thinking decreases'

Play is a great stress-reliever. It is tough to be creative when you are under extreme stress. Of course there are a few famous examples of creativity thriving when pressure is high. Often posited is the ingenuity of the NASA engineers at mission control who, Blue Peter-like, devised a way to get the Apollo 13 astronauts back to Earth using bits of their flight procedure manual and gaffer tape. However, research has found that more commonly, stress kills creativity.

In a recent Yale-Harvard study of creativity, researchers found that, while people under pressure believe themselves to be more creative, their actual results were less creative than when sufficient time was available[37]. Participants in the study were asked to keep a journal explaining how they experienced time pressure on a day-to-day basis, and measuring their ability to think creatively under such pressure. The results demonstrated that as time pressure increased, creative thinking decreased. In addition, the researchers noticed a phenomenon they named a 'pressure hangover'. More time pressure on a certain day didn't just mean less creativity on that day but on the following day too, and this could last two days at least.

Why does this occur? Einstein referred to creativity as 'combinatorial play' because, to his mind, throwing ideas around and seeing how they might collide in interesting ways was a kind of play in itself. Such juggling of concepts and thoughts takes time. There is something random about it and therefore, when time pressure is high, there simply isn't enough time for unusual collisions to occur and new ideas to be created. A clever, original collision might happen within 30 seconds. But the likelihood of such a collision occurring is much greater if more time is given to the exercise.

'A certain amount of stress is good for us... it keeps us motivated, focused and pumped-up'

This is not to say that stress and time pressure is all bad. A certain amount of stress is good for us. 'Eustress' is the term for the good kind of stress that keeps us motivated, focused and pumped-up. Just imagine the feeling of butterflies and adrenaline that circulates around your body when you have been working hard towards a particular end and the time has come to demonstrate what you can do. If you've trained for a half marathon, revised hard for an exam or rehearsed for a live stage performance, you will know this feeling.

But at a certain point, eustress turns in to bad stress and performance suffers – pressure turns to anxiety, focus turns to fuzziness and your raised heart-rate turns to heart-burn.

One hundred years ago, researchers Robert Yerkes and John Dodson demonstrated that efficiency increases when stress increases but only up to a certain point (this is known as the Yerkes-Dodson Curve). New research by Mind/Body expert Herbert Benson[38] has demonstrated that, if stressful activity is immediately ceased as soon as people reach the top of the Yerkes-Dodson Curve and replaced with quiet, rejuvenating activity for a while, the individuals concerned do not become immediately re-stressed when they return to work.

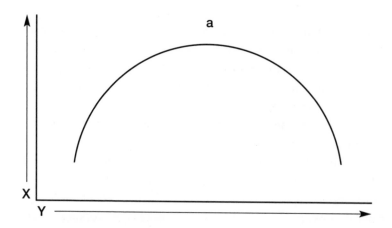

Figure 3: The Yerkes-Dodson Curve.
Y-axis = stress-level.
X-axis = performance/efficiency level.
a = the point at which stress is optimal for top performance.
(Beyond point a, stress-levels are too high and effectiveness begins to fall.)

Herbert Benson has shown that when a calming activity occurs at point *a*, little puffs of nitric oxide are released that give the individual a sense of well-being. At the same time, another phenomenon is observed where individuals have a sudden creative insight, perhaps solving the very problem they were struggling with before they took a break. Individuals are able to return to the previous activity without becoming immediately stressed again (until they reach point *a* again and need to take another break).

In her book *Beyond Love and Work – Why Adults Need to Play*[39], Lenore Terr sings the praises of 'hanging out'. Hanging out is most commonly associated with teenagers and is how their version of play evolves as their overt interest in playing games wanes. Hanging out is actually a creative activity. Terr describes adolescent hanging-out time as time when their minds are idle. Thoughts come and go. Pictures flit in and out. A one-sentence secret is shared. Acquaintances build. Quiet ensues. Lasting friendships take hold.

As adults, some of us manage to create some hanging-out time – at the gym, the coffee shop or the pub. These are opportunities to make friends, let our guard down, smell different smells, be stimulated in different ways. But such time can be built into the working day, too. It may be that skipping work for an afternoon to hang out at the cinema, the park or the zoo could result in better performance at work, along with better ideas.

Play time can also mean gathering inspiration from a variety of seemingly disconnected sources. At Nissan, Hirshberg's team worked for a while on designing a luxury yacht. Although completely foreign to most of them, the process of working on this unusual project inspired them when they returned to building cars. Cross-fertilization occurred, bringing a fresh perspective to the team's day job. Companies that understand creativity encourage their people to explore diverse areas of interest. Attending a lecture on biotechnology might seem irrelevant to you in your job as a postman, but who knows?

They listen

Just as creative organizations allow themselves to be inspired by play and diverse influences, they also have a culture of listening. The options for listening are unlimited – current staff, former staff, prospective staff, those at the top, middle and bottom of the organization, all have something to offer. But listening organizations go further. They develop relationships with customers (including former customers and prospective customers), other stakeholders, even their competition, in order to generate fresh concepts and be ahead of the game.

Future developments don't come from nowhere. They are rooted very firmly in the present and solve problems that exist today. Creative organizations ask, 'Where is the pain? What current problems exist for us, for our customers, for society as a whole?' Successful new products evolve out of technology or systems that already exists. They may fulfil a need that few people realized existed even though it was there all along. It just took some bright spark to notice.

That's why we're not all walking around in silver-foil suits with deeley-boppers on our heads. It might feel futuristic, but aluminium clothing doesn't actually resolve any real challenges we have today.

And how do we know what problems exist? By asking questions and listening to the answers.

Case study – 'Tony'

I went along to this talk about alternative energy because I'm interested in things like that – hydro-power and the new energy technologies.

There were about 50 people there and I thought I would ask a question. I asked the wind energy expert, 'Is there any reason why all the wind turbines you see around are white? Is it for a thermal reason? Is it because if they were black they would expand and cables would become loose or is it for some aesthetic reason?'

And he says, 'Well, they're not really white, are they? They are off-white.'

That's not really what I meant! It was clear he had never asked himself this question. I am always asking questions – that's how I get my ideas. Sometimes the most obvious questions lead to the most interesting realizations. It seems obvious to me to notice things and to ask questions, but maybe it isn't obvious to everyone.

Sometimes the best question is very simple: what isn't working? Increasingly, with the realization that quality of service is a factor in people's buying decisions, most companies have a complaints procedure. Some companies handle complaints very swiftly. However, a listening company gets to the source of complaints, using them to learn how to improve whole systems rather than seeing each problem in isolation.

At SAS, customer complaints and suggestions are collected through their website and over the phone. In addition, the company asks for feedback and suggestions for added features annually through a web-based ballot. Complaints and comments are routed to the appropriate expert and tracked on a database. When the next version of a piece of SAS software is developed, all the recorded glitches are fixed and as many suggestions are incorporated as possible.

The customer plays a central part in the creative process: SAS takes action on about 80 per cent of all requests made.

Andrall Pearson, former president of PepsiCo, knows something about creative organizations. When looking for ways to innovate, he suggests three key areas to ask questions and listen to answers:

- What's already working in the marketplace that you can improve on as well as expand?
- How can you segment your markets differently and gain a competitive advantage in the process?
- How do your business systems compare with those of your competitors?[40]

Such questions and answers are more analytical than beliefs-driven. As a beliefs-driven Hyper-Creative, the idea of incremental improvements, analyzing data and upgrading ideas that already exist might sound rather bland. But actually this is perfect for you. Within your organization are plenty of analytical Hyper-Creatives and analytical non-Hyper-Creatives. There is a vital role for them in this process, which is just further evidence that everyone can contribute to creativity. Peter Drucker says that successful innovation is both conceptual and perceptual[41]. Would-be innovators must also go out and look, ask and listen; successful innovators use both the right and left sides of the brain.

If the innovator is not an individual but a team or a whole organization, different people can perform these different functions – another way you get to focus on your preferences while others focus on theirs.

TURNING THE TITANIC AROUND

It is very exciting to imagine companies based around these principles, isn't it? What would it be like to go to work every day in an environment that celebrated failure, allowed employees to watch *King Kong* at the multiplex in the middle of the afternoon, and where customer complaints were seen as opportunities to listen and improve rather than a chance to blame and get one up on colleagues?

Your company can become this way. The organizations I have referred to have been through a process of change, started by some genius (or a growing constituency of geniuses), who recognized that the company would only keep its competitive advantage if it embraced creativity.

But you don't need to get the whole company behind you in order to use your imaginative abilities to influence working styles. You could just start with the people closest to you. And that's what we'll look at in the next chapter.

CHAPTER TEN

GIVING THE GIFT OF CREATIVITY – PART 2: CREATING CREATIVE PEOPLE

....

No one likes a clever clogs. And maybe that doesn't bother you. But if you are going to coach (and coax) other people to become more creative – for the good of the company and your own mental well-being – you are going to have to do it in such a way that includes your colleagues, as opposed to alienating them.

In the previous chapter, we looked at some of the key elements of creative organizations – they create sparks, they enable the freedom to fail, they make time for play and they listen. But how does an organization get to be that way? Are creative organizations just born like that? Do they go through a massive programme of change in order to become like that? Or does someone start the process from within their team and slowly attitudes shift and change trickles through the rest of the company?

At Nissan, a separate unit was developed on creative principles. SAS did it through trial and error over a period of about three years. You might decide to help your own team first, then demonstrate the benefits of this alternative way of working and help it spread around your company by using your emotional intelligence skills.

STEP 1 – GET IN THE BLACK

In order to start this process you will need to be 'in the black' with your work-mates. What this means, according to Stephen Covey in *The 7 Habits of Highly Effective People*[42], is that you will be in a position where people are willing to listen to you and take your advice. They may not agree with you but they are open to you. When you are in the red in the metaphorical 'emotional bank account', your creative suggestions, no matter how well-meaning, can get you into trouble.

> ### *Case study – 'Kat'*
>
> *I was a technician and I kept finding fault with the way they were running the company. I thought, 'If you were to do it this way, the services we offer would be more attractive to the general public.' And, because I would suggest things like that, I became known as a bossy boots. And the next thing you know I was out the door. And they cheered because I was this bossy boots and I had got the sack. It's just that I see an opportunity and I think, 'Let's take it. It's exciting.' But they didn't like that there.*

Getting into the black is not easy. Some of your Hyper-Creative habits may have tested the patience of your colleagues. They have made allowances for you and, every time they have done that, you have made a withdrawal from the emotional bank account. If you have not done so already you will need to start making deposits. Managing the extremes of your Hyper-Creativity is a start. Crossing the 't's and dotting the 'i's will show your willingness to make the first move. Listening to feedback and acting on it will help too.

Once you have regained the trust of your work-mates, you will need to leave some time for this to bed down. People are sceptical of sudden changes in others and will want to be sure the changes are here to stay.

Your temptation will almost certainly be to dive into this process. As a Hyper-Creative you are probably impatient and want to see change happen yesterday. And perhaps you have already done the groundwork and can get on with step two. Just remember that people won't listen to you if they don't trust you. If you are wondering why your great ideas for change are falling on deaf ears, ask yourself whether you are well and truly in the black.

STEP 2 – WHERE IS THE PAIN?

You need to get your colleagues to buy-in. You want to make changes to the way that the team works and how it makes space for (or is built around) ideas. To achieve this you will need a compelling case that will convince your colleagues there is a problem that needs solving (and it's not enough to tell them that you read it in a book).

What is stopping your team performing even better than it does now? How would a more creative approach get solid bottom-line results and improve emotional well-being and motivation? Where could some changes be made that would dramatically improve performance?

One place I often start is meetings. Most employees spend some of their time in meetings. In some companies, meetings take up most of the day.

Meetings get a bad rap. They are seen as a waste of time, taking staff away from their real work. And the research backs this up. When the CEOs, COOs, CFOs and other senior individuals of 187 companies worldwide with market capitalizations of at least $1 billion were studied by management consultant Michael C. Mankins[43], the majority of executive teams were shown to spend their time discussing issues that had little or no impact on company value (i.e. the bottom line/shareholder value/continuous competitive success).

There were various reasons for this, but two central points in terms of creativity were that meetings weren't structured to produce real decisions and that little time was spent debating strategy (80 per cent of time was devoted to issues accounting for less than 20 per cent of the company's long-term value). Debate about the bigger picture and generation of ideas for the future were marginal. Instead, meetings were largely opportunities for 'information sharing'.

'Meetings are seen as a waste of time... and the research backs this up'

So, during a typical meeting, when does the discussion about ideas and the decision-making take place?

Unfortunately, it is in the few minutes after information has been shared (but before people have had a chance to absorb what the information means) and the close of the meeting.

Some of you may feel that the meetings you attend are already bogged down in debate and discussion. Perhaps, but how many genuinely original, thought-provoking ideas come out of that discussion? How involved do all attendees feel in that process? Is there any structure behind this creative thinking? And, when this part of the process has ended and a decision is made, does everyone feel they have had their say?

Conventional meetings don't work well for everyone. Introvert, analytical thinkers need time to contemplate the information they have received. Until they have done so they cannot be creative. Extrovert, beliefs-driven decision-makers tend to dominate such meetings and, if they are outvoted, go away disillusioned and unconvinced by any decisions that have been taken. Creatives may feel they did not get a chance to really explore options, while practical thinkers may feel unsettled because they are not sure what was decided and what they are now expected to do. Everyone has a different interpretation of what occurred, some are unhappy a decision didn't go their way and others see the decision as tentative or incomplete. As a result nothing (or a mixed message) is relayed to the rest of the team, hindering or preventing action.

Transforming some meetings into creative forums could be a beneficial place to start your campaign to bring ideas generation and creative problem-solving into your workplace.

This might mean specifying the role of each meeting or agenda item. At Cadbury-Schweppes all reading material is sent out five days before an executive meeting, using a standard template where possible so that attendees know where to find the information they need. Analytical thinkers will read the material before, giving them a chance to compose their ideas. Beliefs-driven thinkers should also read the material before (although in my experience they are likely, at best, to skim!). A standard coversheet is provided specifying why people are being asked to read the information (e.g. for information only, for discussion and debate, for a decision and agreement over a course of action). And, where possible, ways are found outside of the meeting to deal with most issues that are purely information sharing.

In addition, some companies separate operational meetings from strategic meetings. This enables them to see how much time they are giving to 'big picture, forward-looking' thinking, and how much they are spending on current issues and fire-fighting. It also helps attendees prepare their minds differently – should I have my 'no-holds-barred' thinking hat on or my 'quick fix' decision-making hat on?

STEP 3 – THE GROUND RULES

Meetings are also a good place to start because they are, at their heart, relatively formal. Introducing a set of ground rules to the way people work in your open-plan office might face some opposition. Colleagues are likely to feel that informal negotiation is the best way to figure out how to work well with one another, but introducing the idea of ground rules to a meeting might gain more approval simply because meetings are seen as artificial anyway.

What ground rules make it safe to create? When I work with teams who want to improve their effectiveness and tap their creative spirit, I encourage them to develop their own boundaries that are unique to their particular environment and that they have agreed to. Starting such a discussion with a provocation such as, 'What would really make it hard to come up with ideas?' can sometimes get clearer answers than, 'What would make it really safe for people to come up with ideas?' Once you know what would make creativity difficult, you can all extrapolate what would make it easier or safer.

Just in case no one knows where to start, here are some ground rules I believe are fundamental:

There is no such thing as a bad idea

As you know, when you are being creative you don't always hit the mark first time. Some ideas will never fly. But once you start censoring yourself you dry up. Permission to say anything that pops in to your head, no matter how silly, unrealistic, expensive, inappropriate or just plain wrong gives everyone the freedom to contribute.

Anyone can contribute anything

Generally, in the car manufacturing industry, new designs are made into a prototype and wheeled out into the car park to be assessed. Traditionally, the only people invited to this event are other designers. It is felt that their input will be valuable – they have specialist insight and can not only identify problems but also suggest solutions. In fact, conventional ground rules state that a criticism can only be made when an alternative solution can be provided. After all, if you can't think of anything better, who are you to criticize?

However, true to form, Jerry Hirshberg at Nissan Design International decided to challenge this convention. He invited anyone to come to a viewing, designers and non-designers alike. And he encouraged 'unconstructive criticism' as well as 'unconstructive enthusiasm'. It was valid to say 'I just don't like it' even if you did not know why or what to do about that.

During the critiquing of one car, the Cocoon, an executive secretary called Cathy Woo spoke out: 'Well, it just looks fat, ugly and dumb to me.'[44] Okay, perhaps a little more tact could have been applied, but Cathy's comments were simply an expression of what everyone was thinking. Her feedback clarified thoughts and the designers went back to the drawing board.

'Valid ideas can come from "invalid" sources'

Because brainstorming generally has a negative connotation, the more you can involve everyone the more you challenge the perception that generating ideas is just for a few expert creative thinkers. Valid ideas can come from 'invalid' sources.

Criticize at the right time
Capturing ideas and challenging those ideas are two separate stages. If an idea is open to challenge immediately it is spoken it is unlikely to survive. Ideas need to be mulled over, honed, developed and tested before they can be rejected. Criticism is vital. But it should only happen once all the ideas are on the table and after everyone is happy that their contribution has been fully explored.

You can criticize the idea but not the person
Our ideas can feel very personal. Therefore criticism of an idea can feel like a personal attack. But as we already know, sparks are a necessary part of the creative process. An environment where everyone is too polite to share their conflicting opinions is unlikely to produce originality. Keeping criticisms focused on the idea, as opposed to extending them to the person, enables all participants to speak honestly and openly.

Agree decision-making criteria
Knowing how and why a decision will be made will not only enable people to focus their ideas but will also help them understand why their ideas may have been rejected. If the decision is going to be made by the majority, then you know what you need to do – win over as many people as you can. If a decision is going to be made

by the boss, likewise you know what you need to do – convince him or her based on whatever kind of answer she or he is looking for (cheapest, quickest, most radical, least challenging etc.). At the time you are establishing the decision-making criteria you might also agree the point at which a decision is final. Until that point there may be justification for discussing and debating the pros and cons of a course of action outside of the meeting. After the decision has been made it is time for action. Your commitment is needed, whether or not the final decision was based on your idea.

No gossip

This relates to the last two points. Creativity does not need to be personal. Once a decision has been made, a sense of cabinet responsibility is required (that is, in government, debate between ministers can openly occur in cabinet meetings but once outside all cabinet members *should* publicly support the collective decision). Therefore there is no place for bickering, gossip, personal insults and the rest. It is to your benefit to keep such negativity out of the creative process. If creativity is associated with this kind of conflict, then the benefits will be overshadowed by the side-effects and your campaign to transform your company's culture will fall at the first hurdle.

Make it work for everyone

You now know the infinite range of working styles that can live within one team. You'll have introverts and extroverts, creative people and practical people, beliefs-driven decision-makers and analytical decision-makers and individuals with a preference for structure or a preference for flexibility. A useful ground rule is that attendees shape the meeting based on what works best for them. Some people will need time to think about this and get back to you. Others will want to refine the meeting structure as you go, tweaking and adapting as they notice a problem. But whatever happens, ensure that everyone is able to fully participate and that the structure of the meeting does not exclude someone with a preference different to your own.

Make it fun

Meetings and fun aren't normally found in the same sentence, but a stagnant meeting environment will lead to stagnant ideas. Hold the meeting somewhere conducive to creative thought, perhaps away from the office. Make it visual and hands-on. Change the dynamic by having people break out into smaller groups. Use your creativity to design a creative meeting.

Stay focused

All the above ground rules may give the impression that meetings should become a free-for-all. Most of the time a meeting has time constraints, and most people have patience constraints. 'Out of the box' thinking has its place. But sometimes 'in the box' thinking is more appropriate and potentially more creative (there is more on this concept later in this chapter). Any idea is valid but it must be focused on the desired outcome.

Hold one another accountable for sticking to the ground rules

You will have different or additional ground rules to these based on what would make your colleagues feel safe to contribute. But ground rules only work when there is a commitment to uphold them. Breaches should be addressed swiftly. If a new ground rule is needed because one of the agreed rules isn't working by all means add it. Just ensure that what you are left with enables everyone to take part in generating ideas and contributing to decisions.

STEP 4 – CHALLENGE ASSUMPTIONS AND ASK CREATIVE QUESTIONS

Once you are in the black, have identified where creative thinking would benefit the team and have some ground rules in place, you all need to start thinking creatively in order to generate ideas.

This comes naturally to you. You probably don't even know how you do it. But to other people on your team, ideas do not come so easily. A better understanding of how to be creative will assist them in taking part in any creative problem-solving.

Edward de Bono, the author of numerous books on creative thinking, uses the term 'provocation' to describe a process where one intentionally sets out to challenge everything we think of as 'normal' or 'realistic'[45].

We make assumptions all the time. We assume we know what 'the reality' is. We assume we have the same reality. We assume we all want the same thing (or we assume we want totally different things). Challenging assumptions can be fruitful territory for generating ideas.

Let's say Jo wants to start a new business. A colleague might say, 'But you can't. Starting a business costs a lot of money and where are you going to get the cash?'

Jo's initial reaction is probably to say, sarcastically, 'Thanks for your support!' But if she were to use this as an opportunity to challenge assumptions she might see the comments differently.

It feels a bit Sesame Street to say this but how many assumptions are in that cynical utterance?

'You can't.' Who says? Why not?

'Starting a business costs money.' Does it? What if starting a business could be done for free? Even if it does cost money, how much are we talking about? Is it necessarily too much? And even if it is expensive, the colleague is assuming Jo doesn't have any money. Maybe she's a secret millionaire.

'Where are you going to get the cash?' If the assumption that Jo needs money and doesn't have it is true, this is a good question. The question can spark creative thinking. Jo could look for venture capital. She could borrow. She could sell her house. She could ask her parents…

When you and your colleagues embark on some creative thinking, a simple question, like 'What are we assuming to be true?', can get your juices flowing. Once the assumptions are on the table, you can begin to challenge them by asking, 'What if this is not true? What would be possible then?'

Asking questions also forms a vital part of creative thinking. In fact creativity can start by asking creative questions because creative answers tend to follow. And creative questions don't need to be complicated. The most basic creative question is 'Why do we do it this way?'

Generally, questions beginning with 'Why...' sound aggressive or accusatory. Just try asking 'Why?' without implying the other person has done something stupid/wrong/inconsiderate. See what I mean?

Questions beginning with 'What...' are less harsh: 'What do we do currently?' or 'What could we do differently?' are often recommended as a way to access wisdom more effectively than 'Why?'.

However, the creative environment has different ground rules (as discussed earlier). 'Why do we do this?', 'Why do we think this?', 'Why do we accept this?' can set up a provocation – a challenge to current assumptions and beliefs.

In his book *Disruption*, advertising guru Jean-Marie Dru writes about the power questions have to challenge conventions[46]. In the advertising world, industries become saddled with conventional ways of approaching different products. Shampoo is sold by emphasizing the effect it has on hair (more lustrous, shiny, thick, straight etc.). Cereal is sold as a breakfast food. Beer is sold by celebrating male bonding and masculine activities (sports mainly, but also the pure pleasure of sitting in the pub with your mates).

But why? Really distinct advertising challenges these conventions. It poses the question 'Why do we do it this way?' and follows up with 'Why can't it be different?'.

Dru gives the example of the Clairol Herbal Essences Organic Shampoo advert. Although it might not be obviously different to other shampoo ads, it breaks with convention by selling the experience in the shower ('a totally organic experience') rather than the resultant luxurious head of hair (although we do always see the final result as well, just in case the audience need a little reassurance).

Sometimes the best question is the most obvious question. And this is where you can encourage less 'naturally creative' souls to contribute to the creative process. A valid role in any thinking session is The Questioner. The Questioner may not know the answers to their questions but they still have a right to ask them.

- 'How would this work?'
- 'What risks are we taking?'
- 'Why is X better than Y?'
- 'Who could help with this?'
- 'What else could we do?'

Typically we might find such questions frustrating, especially if they are an individual's only contribution. We might feel that actual ideas would be more constructive than these simple questions.

But stating the obvious can create sparks just as effectively as throwing ideas into the pot. It is up to us to change the way we respond to these questions rather than restricting the rights of other people to ask them.

STEP 5 – ENCOURAGE AND RECOGNIZE

Inevitably not everyone's ideas will make the final cut. Even with your ground rules firmly in place, people will need to feel their contribution was recognized whether or not their ideas were accepted.

In part, feelings of rejection can be minimized by separating yourself from your ideas (see the ground rules on page 136). When Cathy Woo of Nissan Design International called their car 'ugly', the designers may have felt a twinge of discomfort. Can you imagine how hard it must have been to hear your design described in that way? This was months of work dismissed in a moment.

But the designers must have realized that adding value to their organization as creative individuals and supporting others in exploring their creative abilities meant knowing when to fight and when to move on. They may have found it hard to hear Cathy's comments. But they also knew she was right.

Creativity isn't only about the initial flash of inspiration. Our first idea isn't always our best. The input of other people, their challenging questions, their honest, gut-feeling reactions, their fact-based evidence... all of these things can help us refine and improve our original concept. In a sense it is easy to have a great idea when there are no limitations and when no one else needs to be convinced but you.

Smart creativity is the ability to solve problems, align different perspectives and come up with a solution that appeals to all (or most) of those involved. Often we hear the now clichéd phrase 'out of the box' thinking. But one could argue that 'in the box' thinking is more challenging and more creative. 'In the box' thinking means artificially or realistically setting boundaries for the creative thinking process. One might say, 'Let's only hear ideas that cost less than £10.' Or one might say, 'We only have three people to complete this project. How can we do this when it is normally a job for five people?' Sometimes, putting limitations on creative brainstorming results in better ideas than completely free thinking. And in the real world, a successful idea will be one that works within certain constraints. How does one overcome the very real limitations on a business while still being original? Now, that's creativity.

By mentally separating yourself from your ideas you will be flexible enough to accept and build on feedback. And you will educate those around you to do the same. One reason that people do not share their ideas is fear of criticism and rejection. If you can show that it is possible to share ideas and have them rejected without losing your sense of self-worth, then you can start to change attitudes to creativity and encourage more people to step forward.

Letting go of ownership of an idea also means that people with preferences different to yours can step in and add value. Some people are more suited to refining and enhancing the ideas of others. The initial spark eludes them but once they've seen your idea, their own juices start to flow. Handing on your raw concept at this point can feel like giving your newborn baby to a total stranger. But if this is the point at which you start to lose interest anyway, they are doing you a favour. Reducing your emotional attachment to 'your' idea can release you, enabling you to focus on the new and fresh while other people work your concept into something tangible.

Case study – 'Sophie'

If I have to I can devise procedures and that kind of thing. I can do it because when I put it on my 'to do' list it must have been worthy of being on there. And I get some satisfaction from achieving it. But I would never be able to do it alone. I find someone I enjoy working with who has the skills and preferences I don't have. We make it into a bit of a laugh but I probably look to them to do more 'work' than me. I give as much time and input as you want but I don't like writing or designing a document if it isn't a new way of doing something. I would be there for months writing a Service Level Agreement for example!

At the start of this chapter we learnt about the emotional bank account and it comes into play at this stage too. Reducing your emotional attachment to your ideas is the ideal. But some people will always find this hard to do.

Not everyone will feel their contribution was significant. That's why genuine recognition and acknowledgement of everyone's part in the final decision is so important. It makes a much needed deposit in the bank account, keeping it in the black for the next time creative thinking is required. If someone feels their ideas never make the selection they will start to lose faith in their ability to assist in the process.

But even a 'bad' idea can set up a provocation that leads to a great idea. Perhaps something someone said sparked someone else which sparked someone else and led to the solution. Tracking where the idea started and acknowledging everyone who was part of that chain demonstrates the validity of everyone's presence.

While this kind of recognition may feel over the top and the person receiving it may dismiss it, consistently recognizing a person's contribution in a specific and genuine manner is an innate motivator – it works for almost everyone. Making recognition an integral part of your creative environment will help to balance the inevitable healthy conflict that must occur in order to generate fresh, original, effective ideas.

CHAPTER ELEVEN

SO WHAT HAPPENS NOW?

....

Well done. You read the book! Or most of the book. Or you looked at the chapter headings at least. But well done anyway. You got to the end.

And hopefully by now you've got a pretty good sense of what drives your patterns of behaviour, why you find some activities so effortless while others are such a chore, how to manage some of your extremes more effectively and how to start using your innate creativity to positively affect your own success and the success of your team-mates and your company.

So does that mean you are finished? Well, not quite... Because, of course, knowing what to do and doing it are not the same thing. Your primitive guidance system and your intelligence-based guidance system may not yet be in sync so, while you have the information you need and instinct tells you to *do* something, you still have a choice about whether or not to take action.

My intention with this book was to share some insights about the Hyper-Creative personality and provide some tips and tools to give you options for making changes. Your intention when you picked it up was to do something differently and thereby start getting different results in your professional life (and perhaps in your personal life too).

Perhaps the idea of becoming the most successful person you know was the driver for you. Perhaps you wanted to understand your personality better, so that you could minimize the negative impact it sometimes has, while making the most of your gifts. But I am pretty sure that at the beginning of this process, you were intending to take action as a result of what you learnt.

The time for action is now.

> ## Case study – 'Mike'
>
> *I grew up only imagining one future, which was white collar with academic qualifications, and that was the route to security in life. When I became aware there were people called actors and photographers and sports people, I discounted them as being from another planet. I couldn't imagine any options other than being a lawyer, doctor or accountant.*
>
> *At the age of 29, I walked out on all that with the amazing realization that I didn't have to go into an office and write contracts all day, I could do whatever I fancied...which has led to all sorts of adventures over the last 10 years.*

EXCUSES, EXCUSES

I have worked with professional people who want to upgrade their effectiveness for many years. They want to look inside themselves and gain greater self-awareness. They are committed to continually changing and adapting their leadership style, their communication style and their team-working style, so that they can get the best from themselves and their people. They are inspired by ideas and transformation, and want to know how they can create an environment at work where imagination can flourish.

The motivation to act

There is a difference between *wanting* to achieve a goal and having the *motivation* to achieve a goal. A high level of 'want' is not the same as a high level of motivation. Willingness to change is not enough.

It's that old primitive guidance system versus the intelligence-based system again. In part, what motivates my clients is the fact that they are answerable to someone. They may be doing the right thing for the wrong reason (because their pride is powerful and they don't want to have to tell me they didn't take any action after our workshop), but it doesn't really matter as long as they make decisions and take actions. And, as they get used to doing this, they change their habits and embed new ways of working and behaving so that, after a while, they don't need to trick themselves into doing the right thing any more. They do the right thing by habit. They have retrained their primitive guidance system.

I remember hearing a talk by Steve Redgrave, the multi-gold-medal-winning rower. After he retired

> **'They may be doing the right thing for the wrong reason, but it doesn't really matter'**

he still sometimes found himself, as if on auto-pilot, driving to the training centre. Years of making the same journey every day had become hard-wired. When asked how he motivated himself to work so hard for so many years he replied that it was just habit. He was no longer making conscious choices every day. His primitive guidance system had kicked in and, instinctively, he just found himself training hard, day after day after day, without ever questioning his action... much like the squirrel storing nuts for winter.

Our intelligence-based guidance system provides numerous reasons for delaying action:

- 'I'm too busy right now. When things calm down I will get started.'
- 'I've just started a new job. I'll settle down first and then think about addressing my Hyper-Creativity.'
- 'I'm leaving my job soon. I'll start afresh in the new place.'

- 'I need to do a bit more research before I'll be ready to make actual changes.'
- 'I just can't be bothered. I was excited by the idea at the start but, typical me, I've become bored with it now.'

What excuses is your Sergeant Major Barker coming up with to distract you from making real, practical changes?

Back in the 1950s, the granddaddy of motivation theory, Frederick Hertzberg[47], carried out a number of studies into what circumstances motivate people to take action. Most people who were asked said that working conditions, pay, job security, relationships with colleagues and company policies were vital. They felt that if these were poor, their motivation would drop and their performance would be negatively affected.

Because this is what most people believe demotivates them, companies spend large amounts of money trying to improve these conditions. They offer financial bonuses. They spend money on squashy sofas in the newly revamped café area. They encourage niceness between individuals. But, since Hertzberg's time, it has been realized that these factors (termed 'hygiene factors') do not actually motivate. They need to be satisfactory, otherwise they will demotivate, but fixing them does not have the opposite, positive impact. In fact, at best it just leads to less dissatisfaction, not greater motivation.

So, what does motivate? What turns a high level of want into action? Hertzberg (and many others since) have concluded that there are six intrinsic motivators which, once basic conditions at work are satisfactory, can be relied upon to improve motivation and performance:

1. Interest in the work itself.
2. A sense of responsibility.
3. A sense of achievement.
4. Recognition.
5. The prospect for advancement within the organization or industry.
6. The opportunity for personal/professional growth.

In order to take action on those aspects of this book that you feel will offer you the most benefit, it will help if satisfactory hygiene factors are in place. But as long as you blame peripherals (e.g. not enough time, they don't pay me enough to do this, I need to tidy my filing cabinet first...), the circumstances will never be right.

To really motivate yourself into taking action, you will need a combination of elements. Answering the following five questions will help you identify what these are for you:

1. Who will support me?
2. Where is the pain for me? And what is the pay-off for resolving this pain?
3. What do I actually want to do differently? What would I enjoy doing differently?
4. What intrinsic motivators will keep me going as I hit a hurdle?
5. How can I trick myself into doing the right thing... even if it is for the wrong reason?

As you will have noticed, many of these questions have cropped up already in the preceding pages. But, by way of a reminder, let's look at them again:

WHO WILL SUPPORT ME?

You can start building your Success Squad immediately. If you already have people in mind or have been informally using people in this way already, now is the time to formalize those relationships. If not, now is the time to start looking outside your immediate sphere for people who can form part of this team.

Exactly what you need them to do will depend on your own preferences. A priority might be someone to take care of your paper-work. Alternatively, you may feel that being able to talk ideas through with someone who will also hold you accountable, works well for you.

The reason the Success Squad is your first action is simple: as soon as you tell people that you are working on your Hyper-

Creativity and explain how you plan to do that, you have made a public commitment. Few of us will enjoy letting other people down. You've tricked yourself into doing the right thing – getting started on making changes – even if it is for the wrong reason.

This also plays in to Hertzberg's motivation theory. When people are involved in what you are doing they will also recognize and praise your achievements. Remember, Success Squad members should be people who are committed to your success and interested in you. Every time you take a step forward and tell them about it, you will receive recognition and acknowledgement, which will feed your motivation.

WHERE IS THE PAIN FOR ME? AND WHAT IS THE PAY-OFF FOR RESOLVING THIS PAIN?

Earlier in the book, 'Where is the pain?' was identified as a powerful question for encouraging other people in your team or organization to incorporate creative thinking into their business methodology. It means that creative thinking addresses real, current problems and therefore immediately adds value. And, of course, you can use this question to help you get focused, too.

Whether you occasionally experience yourself as Hyper-Creative, or the negatives of being Hyper-Creative rule your life the majority of the time, at some level you are hurting your chances of even greater success. How exactly are you sabotaging yourself? Where is the pain? And what could you gain by minimizing this aspect of your personality?

Remember, at no point have I recommended trying to change your preferences. Your preferences can work wonderfully as a recipe for success and I hope you feel increasingly proud of what your natural talents can bring to your organization. Just have an awareness of where they work less well and how, by simply managing some elements better, you can turn your natural gifts into a dynamic force.

Looking at mood swings and your internal dialogue could be useful here. And in Hertzberg's terms, the pay-off could well be advancement through your organization or your industry.

WHAT DO I ACTUALLY WANT TO DO DIFFERENTLY? WHAT WOULD I ENJOY DOING DIFFERENTLY?

We are most highly motivated around activities we enjoy. As you have been reading the preceding pages you'll have underlined certain ideas, scribbled notes in the margin and developed your own spin-off strategies sparked by something that resonated with you. These are great places to start. These are the ideas that excite you most. Strategies that feel like a huge effort won't be sustainable. When you are deciding what to do differently, choose those strategies that don't feel like hard work.

WHAT INTRINSIC MOTIVATORS WILL KEEP ME GOING AS I HIT A HURDLE?

As mentioned many times, recognition is an important motivator for Hyper-Creatives, particularly extrovert Hyper-Creatives who have no problem being publicly acknowledged for their good work. If you are more introvert, you may need to educate those around you (perhaps your Success Squad members) about how you like to be recognized. Public praise may not be as powerful for you as a personal email or card.

We tend to feel embarrassed about being acknowledged. This is particularly true when we are acknowledged for doing something that comes naturally to us. It is as though we are only worthy of praise if we have struggled. However, the whole concept behind the idea of work-style preferences is that you can have a career in which you focus largely on types of work that you enjoy and are innately suited to. Get used to being praised. It will help you make the biggest changes you want to make, focus your ideas and enable you to see projects through to completion.

Case study – 'Sophie'

Recently I worked on a project that was almost perfect for me. Of course, there were mundane bits, but overall I could create and devise the plan and do it however I wanted. It was a really tight timescale – we only had a month to do it so it was go, go, go. My energy could be sustained for that short period of time because I could see the finishing line the whole time.

There was a lot of travel, going to other sites and meeting new people. That was quite a bonus for me. It got me out and about. I was working on some changes to my 'style' of communication and relationship building and I was able to test out a different style with people who didn't already know me. It almost made it into a game.

HOW CAN I TRICK MYSELF INTO DOING THE RIGHT THING... EVEN IF IT IS FOR THE WRONG REASON?

You are getting used to your patterns now. You are starting to see when you become jaded with an idea, when you are about to hit an emotional down cycle, which activities energize you and which activities drain you.

The greater your level of awareness the more accurate your choice of trick will be. Is this a time when the 'Leading the horse to water' strategy is the best tool (see page 109)? Or is it time to get the Emergency Crash Procedure out (see page 102)?

Until now success has been somewhat accidental. But, as covered earlier, really creative businesses analyze success just as rigorously as they analyze failure. Looking back at times when you have seen projects through will give you useful clues as to the most effective tricks for you. Instead of leaving it to chance, be proactive in your efforts to do the right thing, even if it is just because your reward is a chocolate hobnob.

FINAL THOUGHTS

I have an admission to make. It has not been easy to write this final chapter. As a Hyper-Creative myself, I believe I have experienced every symptom of the condition in the process of writing this book: initial inspiration; the joy of getting started; finding myself in a routine; feeling like it was never going to be finished because there seemed so much to do; getting a grip and getting a second wind; seeing the end in sight and pushing myself (with the help of my Success Squad members) over the finishing line.

Even with all the tips and tricks at my fingertips, even with Hyper-Creativity at the forefront of my mind, my habitual cycle was very much in evidence.

It occurs to me that this might always be the case. After all, our preferences are not going to change. We will always prefer the start – the fresh, shiny, new idea. But by addressing the ways in which those preferences manifest themselves more negatively, we can acknowledge our own tendency to get distracted, disillusioned or just plain bored, and put structures in place to ensure that this no longer really matters.

In my case, this approach enabled me to finish writing this book. Perhaps you have a similar project on which you wish to pilot these techniques. Or maybe there isn't anything quite so concrete to begin with, so you'll have to apply these ideas more generally to aspects of your work.

I believe the benefits of doing this, in terms of your success and fulfilment, are huge. As you start to sculpt your life around your preferences, the opportunities to shine will be numerous. Your Success Squad and other tricks will provide you with a safety net to catch you at times when you slip into old habits... And then there is nothing stopping you from becoming the most successful, satisfied and (if you like) self-satisfied person you know.

ENDNOTES

Introduction
1. © Reproduced by kind permission of TMS Development International Ltd.

Chapter One
2. Myers-Briggs Type Indicator and MBTI are trademarks or registered trademarks of the Myers-Briggs Type Indicator Trust in the United States and other countries.

Chapter Two
3. Julie Coultas, 'Playing It Up', *Baby and Toddler Gear* (November/December 2005)
4. E. Paul Torrance and Kathy Goff 'Fostering Academic Creativity in Gifted Students' (www.kidsource.com/kidsource/content/academic_creativity.html#credits)
5. *Arts & Business* (July 2005) (www.aandb.org.uk/render.aspx?siteID=1&navIDs=1,9,339)
6. Richard Florida and Jim Goodnight, 'Managing for Creativity', *Harvard Business Review* (July/August 2005), p126
7. Sir John Harvey Jones, *Making it Happen – Reflections on Leadership*, 4th Edition (Fontana, 1989), p54

Chapter Three
8. Carl G. Jung, *Psychological Types*, 1923 (Princeton University Press, 1971), pp330–405
9. Roger R. Pearman and Sarah C. Albritton, *I'm Not Crazy, I'm Just Not You* (Davies-Black Publishing, 1997), p7
10. Mike Southon and Chris West, *The Boardroom Entrepreneur* (Random House Business Books, 2005), p22
11. Pearman and Albritton, *I'm Not Crazy, I'm Just Not You*, p7
12. Kay Redfield Jamison, *Touched With Fire* (Free Press Paperbacks, 1993), p85
13. N.C. Andreasen, 'Creativity and Mental Illness: Prevalence rates in writers and their first-degree relatives', *American Journal of Psychiatry* (1987), p1290
14. Abraham Zaleznik, 'Managers and Leaders – Are They Different?', *Harvard Business Review* (January 2004), p74
15. Rachel Welch, 'The Romance of the Gut', *Harvard Business Review* (January 2006), p40

Chapter Five
16. Susan Jeffers, *Feel the Fear and Do It Anyway – How To Turn Your Fear And Indecision Into Confidence And Action* (Arrow Books, 1991), p57

17. Jeffers, *Feel the Fear and Do It Anyway – How To Turn Your Fear And Indecision Into Confidence And Action*, p194

Chapter Six

18. Redfield Jamison *Touched With Fire*, p5
19. Redfield Jamison, *Touched With Fire*, p51
20. J. P. Guilford, 'Traits of Creativity' in H.H. Anderson (Ed.), *Creativity and its Cultivation* (New York: Harper, 1959), pp142–161
21. Leslie A. Marchand (Ed.), 'Letter to Annabella Milbanke, 29 November 1813', *Byron's Letters and Journals*, Volume Three (London: John Murray, 1973-1982), p179
22. Stephen Covey, *7 Habits of Highly Effective People* (Simon & Schuster 1993), p82

Chapter Seven

23. Daniel Goleman, Richard Boyatzis and Annie McKee, *The New Leaders: Transforming the Art of Leadership into the Science of Results* (Little, Brown, 2002) p37. For the basic theory, see Goleman, *Working with Emotional Intelligence* (New York: Bantam Books, 1998)
24. Spencer Johnson, *Who Moved My Cheese – An Amazing Way to Deal With Change In Your Work and In Your Life* (Vermilion, 1999)
25. Jerry Hirshberg, *The Creative Priority* (Harper Business Press, 1998), p16
26. Southon and West, *The Boardroom Entrepreneur*, p44
27. Hirshberg, *The Creative Priority*, p39

Chapter Eight

28. Steve Levinson and Pete Greider, *Following Through – a Revolutionary New Model for Finishing Whatever You Start* (Kensington, 1998), p41
29. Levinson and Greider, *Following Through – a Revolutionary New Model for Finishing Whatever You Start*, p116
30. Levinson and Greider, *Following Through – a Revolutionary New Model for Finishing Whatever You Start*, p142

Chapter Nine

31. Hirshberg, *The Creative Priority* p16
32. Larry Huston and Nabil Sakkab, 'Connect and Develop: Inside Procter & Gamble's New Model For Innovation', *Harvard Business Review* (March 2006), p58
33. Southon and West, *The Boardroom Entrepreneur*, p 25
34. Richard Florida and Jim Goodnight, 'Managing for Creativity', *Harvard Business Review* (July/August 2005), p124

35. Thomas Watson Snr, from Ralph Keyes and Richard Farson, 'The Failure Tolerant Leader', *Harvard Business Review* (August 2002), p64

36. Keyes and Farson, 'The Failure Tolerant Leader', p67

37. Teresa M. Amabile, Constance N. Hadley and Steven J. Kramer, 'Creativity under the gun' *Harvard Business Review* (August 2002), p52

38. Herbert Benson, 'Are you Working Too Hard?' *Harvard Business Review* (November 2005), p55

39. Lenore Terr, *Beyond Love and Work – Why Adults Need to Play* (Scribner, New York 1999), p147

40. Andrall E. Pearson, 'Tough Minded Ways To Get Innovative', *Harvard Business Review* (August 2002), p117

41. Peter Drucker, 'The Discipline of Innovation', *Harvard Business Review* (August 2002), p102

Chapter Ten

42. Covey, *The 7 Habits of Highly Effective People*, p188

43. Michael C. Mankins, 'Stop Wasting Valuable Time', *Harvard Business Review* (September 2004), p58

44. Hirshberg, The Creative Priority, p58

45. Edward de Bono. *Lateral Thinking: Fast Track to Creativity* (Advanced Practical Thinking Training Inc, 1999), p83

46. Jean-Marie Dru, *Disruption – overturning conventions and shaking up the marketplace* (Wiley, 1996), pp65–66

Chapter Eleven

47. Frederick Hertzberg 'One More Time: How do you motivate employees? *Harvard Business Review* (January 2003), p90

ABOUT THE AUTHOR

Blaire Palmer is one of the UK's leading Creative Thinking Partners and Executive Coaches.

Formerly a BBC journalist, Blaire now specialises in brainstorming, creative strategic thinking and problem solving. Her clients are major corporations, entrepreneurs and individuals who, like her, strive to bring real creative solutions into business and realise their own innate creative ability.

Blaire is also a columnist, public speaker and regular guest on BBC Radio.

For more information about Blaire's work or to find out about her courses and workshops, visit her website at www.blairepalmer.com.

INDEX

ACKNOWLEDGEMENTS

Completing this book has been quite an achievement, not only for me, but for the people around me. I have been hugely fortunate to have in my life some fantastic people who help me bring my ideas to fruition and I take this opportunity to acknowledge their support:

I'd like to thank my agents Charlotte Howard and Chelsey Fox for seeing the potential in me and my ideas and trusting me to write this book. Also, thank you to Jo Hemmings, Gareth Jones and Kate Parker at New Holland for 'getting' Hyper-Creativity and ensuring that I dotted all the 'i's and crossed all the 't's.

My appreciation goes to Susan, Jan and the team at TMSDI, Tad Dearden at *Harvard Business Review* and Dan Goleman. Thanks also to my clients, who provided me with hours of fascinating discussion and debate, and my case studies, who were a joy to spend time with.

I couldn't have run my business while writing this book (or at any other time!) without Julia Blower, Sue Brackley and Ros Munton who not only perform miracles with my paperwork but seem genuinely interested in discussing my ideas with me.

Thanks to Ginny Baillie, my coach, for passively/aggressively making sure I submitted the proposal and for her constant enthusiasm and support. I owe Rachel Turner for the concept of the 'Sergeant Major' and express my gratitude to my great friend Katie Rowland and the Bravehearts – Sue Ingram, Pete Bernard and Julie French for their frankness, honesty and interest.

Miscellaneous thanks goes to my amazing friends Heather Beresford, Nancy Brown, Helen Bushby, Sharon Charlton-Thomson, Rich Chappell, Jennifer Chevalier, Phil Gayle, Suzy Greaves, Jim Lawless, Sarah Penny and Paul Rogers, for their friendship over the years, their suggestions and for being an inspiration to me.

Finally, thanks to my parents for their unquestioning belief in me (even when things looked decidedly rocky), my sister Lindsey for being on the end of the phone 24 hours a day armed with something funny to say and to my boyfriend Paul, whose confidence in me never wanes.